Cur toro viduo iaces?

Why lie on an empty bed?

SENECA *PHAEDRA* 448

Scis te id maxime velle

You know you want to.

fatum est!

It's fate!

APUD ME?

My place then?

ME COMMOVE
ME REFRIGERA
ME EXPLE

Thrill Me,
Chill Me,
Fulfil Me.

Nocte una quivis vel deus esse potest

One night like that can make any man a god.

PROPERTIUS 2.15.40

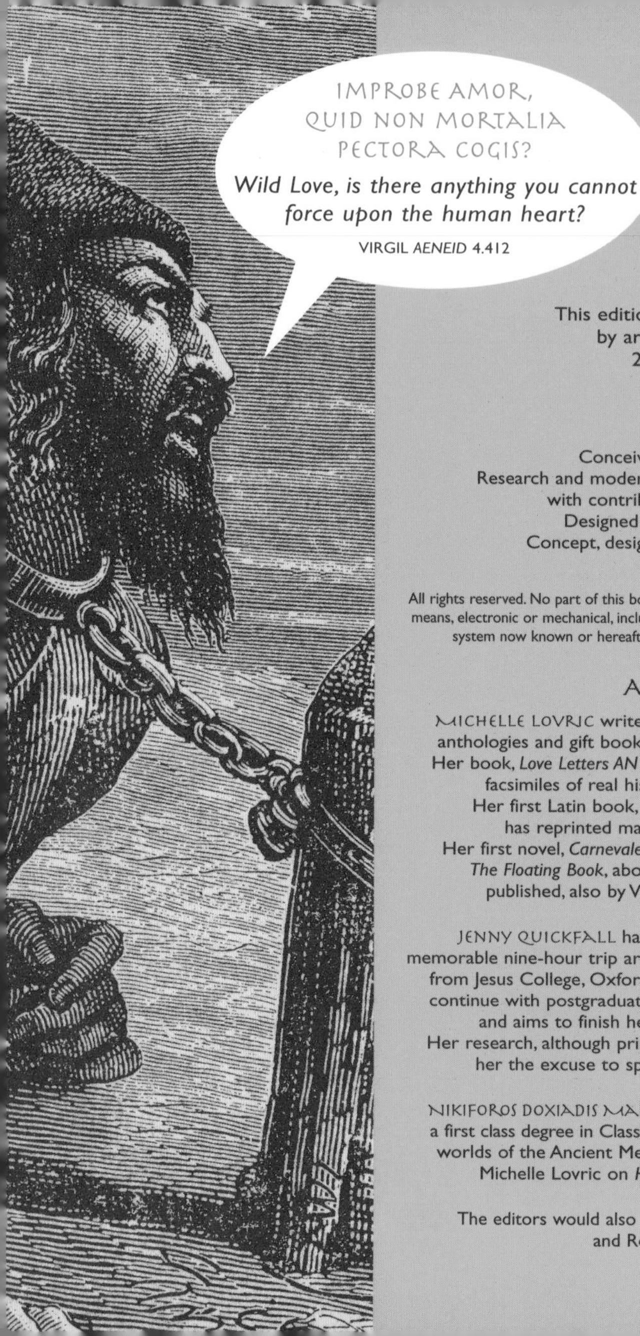
IMPROBE AMOR,
QUID NON MORTALIA
PECTORA COGIS?
Wild Love, is there anything you cannot force upon the human heart?
VIRGIL *AENEID* 4.412

This edition published by Barnes & Noble, Inc,
by arrangement with Michelle Lovric
2003 Barnes & Noble Books
ISBN 0-7607-5050-5

10 9 8 7 6 5 4 3 2 1

Conceived and compiled by Michelle Lovric
Research and modern translations by Michelle Lovric, Jenny Quickfall
with contributions from Nikiforos Doxiadis Mardas
Designed by Michelle Lovric and Lisa Pentreath

Printed in China by Imago

ABOUT THE EDITORS...

MICHELLE LOVRIC writes, researches, translates and designs unique illustrated anthologies and gift books, many with unusual and decorative novelty features. Her book, *Love Letters AN ANTHOLOGY OF PASSION*, featuring three-dimensional facsimiles of real historical letters, was a *New York Times* best-seller. Her first Latin book, *How to Insult, Abuse and Insinuate in Classical Latin*, has reprinted many times, with a total of 100,000 copies sold. Her first novel, *Carnevale*, was published by Virago in 2001. Her second novel, *The Floating Book*, about the poems of the Latin love lyricist Catullus, is published, also by Virago, in the UK and HarperCollins in the USA.

JENNY QUICKFALL has been titillated by the Classical world ever since a memorable nine-hour trip around ancient Pompeii aged ten. She graduated in Classics from Jesus College, Oxford in 1999, and was inspired by the late Don Fowler to continue with postgraduate research. She teaches part-time at Exeter University and aims to finish her PhD at the University of Birmingham in 2004. Her research, although primarily on the less amorous parts of Ovid, has afforded her the excuse to spend much of her time with the Latin love poets.

NIKIFOROS DOXIADIS MARDAS graduated from the University of Cambridge with a first class degree in Classics and has been immersed in the physical and academic worlds of the Ancient Mediterranean throughout his life. He collaborated with Michelle Lovric on *How to Insult, Abuse and Insinuate in Classical Latin*.

The editors would also like to thank Nancy Starr, Bart Stoner, Sally Fitzharris and Roger Davies for their contributions.

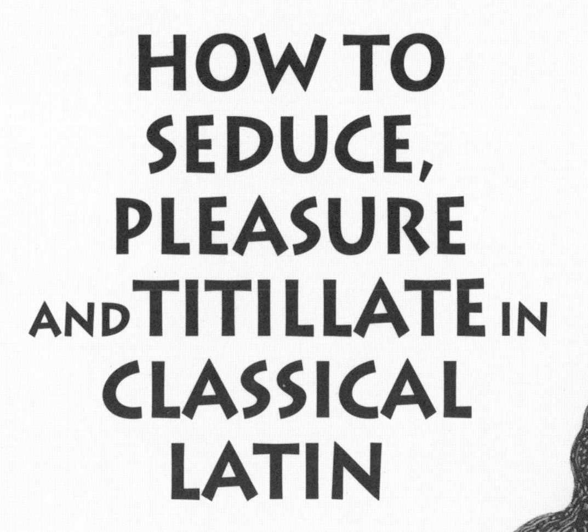

HOW TO SEDUCE, PLEASURE AND TITILLATE IN CLASSICAL LATIN

NAM QUIS CONCUBITUS
VENERIS QUIS GAUDIA NESCIT?
QUIS VETAT IN TEPIDO MEMBRA CALERE TORO?
IPSE PATER VERI DOCTOS EPICURUS AMARE
IUSSIT, ET HOC VITAM DIXIT HABERE ΤΈΛΟΣ

Who doesn't know about love-making and the joys of Venus?
Who can't heat themselves up in a warm bed?
Epicurus the father of truth ordered the wise to love,
proclaiming this to be the "climax" of life.

PETRONIUS *SATYRICON* 132

QUAE DANT QUAEQUE NEGANT,
GAUDENT TAMEN ESSE ROGATAE

Whether they say yes or no, women like to be asked.

OVID *ARS AMATORIA* 1.345

HOW TO SEDUCE, PLEASURE AND TITILLATE IN CLASSICAL LATIN

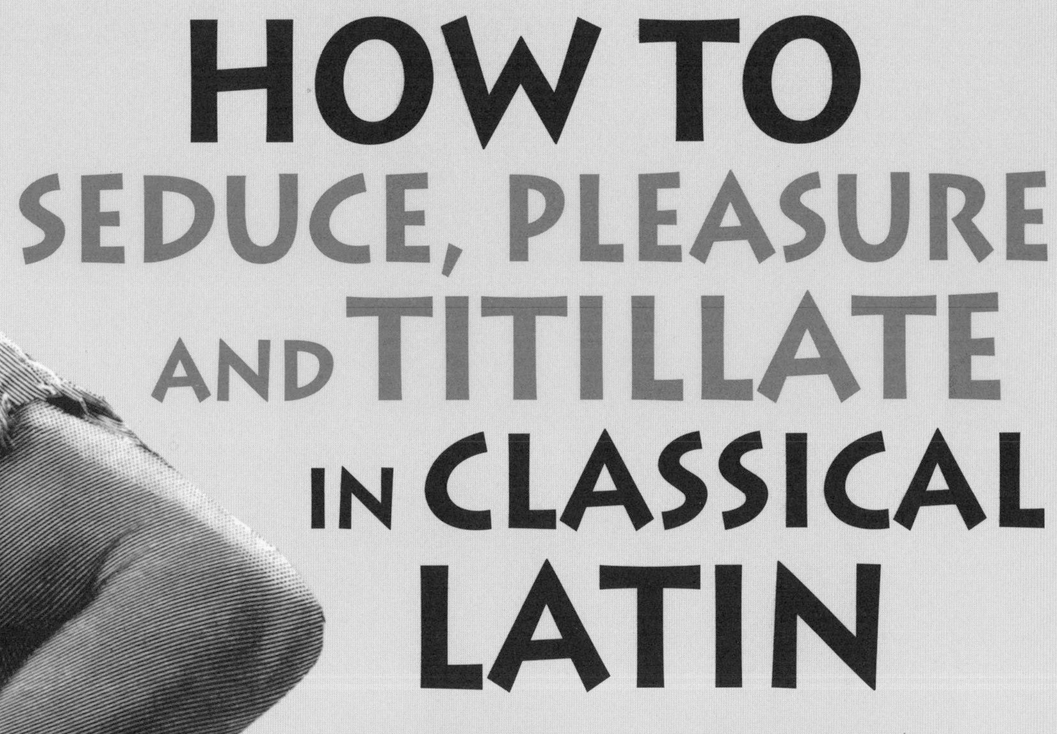

MICHELLE LOVRIC & JENNY QUICKFALL

BARNES & NOBLE BOOKS
NEW YORK

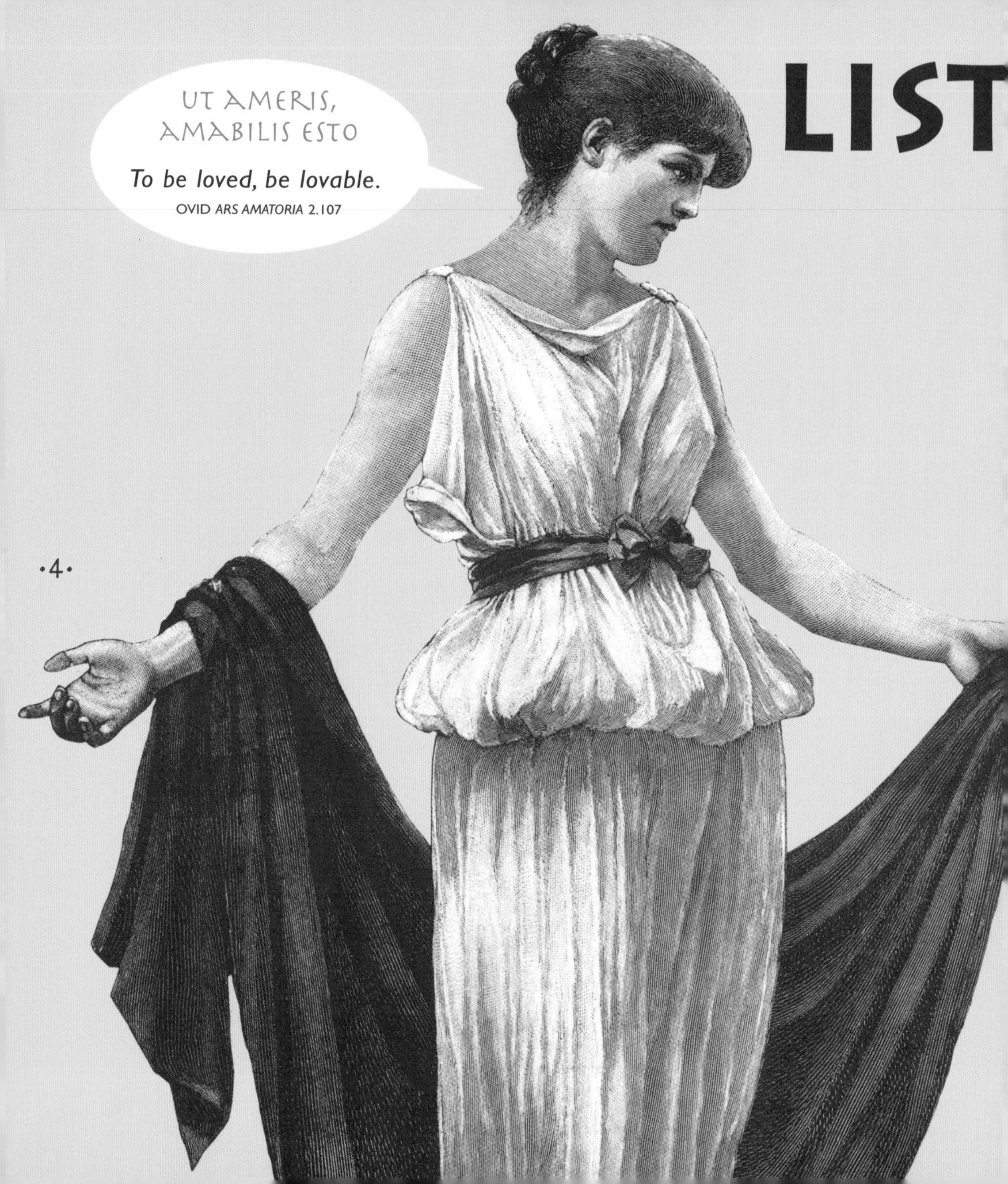
UT AMERIS,
AMABILIS ESTO
To be loved, be lovable.
OVID ARS AMATORIA 2.107
LIST
•4•

OF CONTENTS

IT'S LOVE... IT'S WAR

MILITIAE SPECIES AMOR EST

Love is a kind of war.

OVID *ARS AMATORIA* 2.233

MILITAT OMNIS AMANS,
ET HABET SUA CASTRA CUPIDO

Every lover is a soldier
and Cupid has his own barracks.

OVID *AMORES* 1.9.1

ISTE LASCIVUS PUER ET RENIDENS
TELA QUAM CERTO MODERATUR ARCU

That naughty grinning boy aims his arrows from an unerring bow.

SENECA *PHAEDRA* 277-8

EN EGO CONFITEOR! TUA SUM NOVA PRAEDA, CUPIDO;
PORRIGIMUS VICTAS AD TUA IURA MANUS.

OK, Cupid, I give in – I'm your new prisoner-of-war.
I'm coming out with my hands up.

OVID *AMORES* 1.2.19-20

OMNIA VINCIT AMOR; ET NOS CEDAMUS AMORI

Love conquers all; let us too surrender to love.

VIRGIL *ECLOGUES* 10.69

PRONA TIBI VINCI CUPIENTEM VINCERE PALMA EST

It's an easy prize to conquer someone who wants to be conquered.

OVID *AMORES* 3.14.47

NUMQUAM TE PRIUS VIDI: NUMQUAM TALIS VULTUS OBLIVISCERER

I've never seen you before: I would never forget a face like that.

TE LAESISTI UBI DE OLYMPO CECIDISTI?

Did it hurt when you fell down from Olympus?

FACERE NON POSSUM QUIN PULCHRITUDINE TUI ANIMI PERCUTIAR

But I couldn't help being struck by your inner beauty.

TUUS/TUA MARITUS/UXOR/AMICUS/AMICA FELIX CANIS EST

Your husband/wife/boyfriend/girlfriend is a lucky dog.

IMMO! NON POSSUM CREDERE TE NEMINEM HABERE

No! I can't believe you're single!

EGO ETIAM. NONNE MIRACULUM EST?

Me too. It's amazing, isn't it?

NONNE ERGO RESILIS?

You must be on the rebound then?

IMMO? EXPECTASNE
ILLUM PERFECTUM /ILLAM PERFECTAM?

No? Just waiting for Mr/Ms Perfect?

UBI FUISTI TOTAM MEAM VITAM?

Where have you been all my life?

SIVE ALIQUA
EST OCULOS IN SE
DEIECTA MODESTOS, UROR

A girl who keeps her eyes coyly lowered drives me crazy.

OVID *AMORES* 2.4.11-12

CRESCIT ENIM
ASSIDUE SPECTANDO CURA
PUELLAE:IPSE ALIMENTA SIBI
MAXIMA PRAEBET AMOR

Love for a girl grows with gazing at her: the desire feeds itself.

PROPERTIUS 3.21.3-4

LOVE
SEES
...
LOVE
WANTS

DE TE, ERGO, MIHI NARRA
So, tell me about you.

STUPEFACTUS/STUPEFACTA SUM
I'm gobsmacked.

NOMEN MEUM?
MEI AMICI ME CROESUM/ADONEM/
APHRODITEM/CLEOPATRAM NOMINANT
My name? Well, my friends call me Croesus/Adonis/Aphrodite/Cleopatra.

ITA VERO, MEUS EST ILLE AQUAEDUCTUS
Yes, that's my aqueduct over there.

MEUS ALTER CURRUS QUADRIGAE EST
(I.E. MAXIMUM ROMAN HORSEPOWER)
And my other chariot is a Porsche.

QUICQUID FACIES NOCTE CRASTINA?
Do you have plans tomorrow night?

TESSERAS AD LUDOS HABEO
I have tickets to the Races ...

LOVE FINDS A WAY

STRATAGEMS FOR THE NEW CLASSICAL LOVER

Ovid's *Ars Amatoria*, published in 2 BC, provides much detailed advice that still holds true. Some of his attitudes are surprisingly modern, not to say cynical, but in his lyrical love poetry Ovid shows that he is one of true love's great devotees. In this chapter, Ovid's advice is translated into English, but useful – and reusable – modern phrases are provided in Latin in a separate panel on the facing page.

First, rest assured that all women can be caught, just spread your nets.

1.269-70

Even the law courts (who would've believed it?) are good for finding love.

1.79

Do your hunting especially in the curved theatres.

1.89

Banquets, when the tables are set, provide a way in.

1.229

A second husband is often found at the first husband's funeral.

3.431

If she's strolling through the spacious colonnade,
loiter there for a friendly chat.

1.491-2

The spacious chariot-racing stadium has many
suitable opportunities.

1.136

When she tells you
to meet her somewhere
drop everything and run!
2.225-6

Sit right next to your lady – no-one will stop you –
and snuggle up cheek to cheek as far as you can.
It's good that the rows force proximity, like it or not.

1.139-41

Make sure you make an effort to ask whose horses are coming along
and quickly shift your support to whomever she favours.

1.145-6

If, as happens, a speck of dust falls onto your girl's lap,
flick it off. In fact, flick it off even if there is no dust.

1.149-51

If her cloak hangs too low and trails on the ground,
gather it up and hold it attentively off the dirty earth.

1.153-4

Keep a look out behind to make sure whoever's
sitting there isn't kneeing her in her soft back.

1.157-8

Little things please frivolous minds: many have found it
worthwhile deftly to arrange a cushion for her.

1.159-60

Although you're shivering yourself,
make sure you warm her hand in your freezing lap.

2.213-14

When the tables are cleared away and the party leaves ...
slip in among the crowd, sidle softly up to her, tug on her clothes
and nudge her foot with yours.

1.603, 605-6

Add the gifts of personality to physical good looks.

2.112

Skilful kindness especially captures hearts.

2.145

Take the trouble to learn a couple of languages.

2.122

Let love find a way in disguised as friendship.

1.720

Make your move when she's on the rebound:
then make sure by your efforts that she gets her revenge.

1.365-6

Stop yourself especially from pointing out her faults;
it's useful to turn a blind eye.

2.641-2

Don't ask how old she is or under which consul she was born.

2.663-4

Make sure she thinks you thunderstruck by her beauty.

2.296

If she's parted her hair, praise her parting.

2.303

Get up when she does and sit down when she does.

1.503

If she's playing a game and throwing ivory dice, deliberately misthrow.

2.203-4

If you can sing, sing; if you can hold your drink, drink.

2.506

Trace playful come-ons in the thin, spilt wine.

1.571

Criticize what she criticizes, approve what she approves, say what she says, deny what she denies. Laugh when she laughs and remember to cry when she cries. Let her rule on your facial expressions.

2.199-202

Let her always be seeing you and listening to you: let her see your face night and day.

2.347-8

Let your eyebrows and gestures speak volumes.

1.500

Hold her gaze with a gaze that confesses its passion.

1.573

Tears are useful: tears can move stone.

1.659

If tears fail (for they don't always come on cue) dampen your eyes with a wet hand.

1.661-2

Make lots of promises: what harm can it do to make promises?

1.443

Stay deodorized and get a glow from exercise.

1.513

Don't let a rude goat in under your armpits.

3.193

Don't be lazy and let your teeth grow black.

3.197

Don't let your legs get rough with bristling hair!

3.194

Choose a colour that's a dead certainty:
they don't all suit everyone.

3.187-8

Even the "natural" look suits many.

3.153

Pride in your looks will make them better.

3.105

And your face should be washed in the morning.

3.198

If real blood doesn't bring colour to your cheeks,
make them blush artificially.

3.200

Pencil in your eyebrows artificially.

3.201

There's no shame in shading your eyes with thin ash.

3.203

But don't let your lover catch you with your make-up bag out on the table: it helps you to look natural.

3.209

While you're putting your face on let us think you're asleep: it's better to see the finished product.

3.225-6

Fake a headache now and then.

AMORES 1.8.73

Come to parties fashionably late and make an elegant entrance when the lamps have been lit ... you'll appear stunning to those who're tipsy and the night will hide your faults.

3.751, 753-4

Make him hope and fear together.

3.477

Make sure he doesn't get complacent through lack of competition.

AMORES 1.8.95

LONELY

POETA PUERILIS PETIT MUSAM SENIOREM QUAE ANIMAM VIOLET, HENDECASYLLABOS INFLET, STYGIO FATO EUM ERIPIAT. SUA BASIS NECESSARIA EST

Boyish poet seeks older Muse to ravish his soul, pump up his hendecasyllables and save him from Stygian gloom. Must have own pedestal.

LIBERA TUAM TIGREM! VIR GLADITORIUS, QUI AMAT VEHEMENTER DISPUTARE, **VO** FEMINAE AD PUGNAS AMATORIAS

Bring out the Tigress in you! Gladiatorial type, likes a good argument, seeks a woman for amatory combat.

OMNIA PRAETER PUELLAM. PATRICIUS DIVES, QUI VILLAS ROMANAS BAIANASQUE TRANSPADANASQUE POSSIDET PETIT FEMINAM PERSPICACEM QUAE FAMOSAM VITAM SECUM AGAT ET NEPOTES PRAEBEAT. ANTE ID. MART. RESPONDE

Everything but the girl. Wealthy patrician with homes in Rome, Baiae and Transpadine Gaul seeks discriminating woman to share his celebrity lifestyle and found a dynasty. Please apply before the Ides of March.

ADMISSARIUS APERTUS, SICILIANUS, LIBERTUS, LIBERTAM PETIT AD VOLUPTATEM MUTUAM ET HONOREM. OMNES HARPYIAE ABSINT!

Sincere Sicilian Stallion, freedman, seeks freedwoman for mutual pleasure and advancement. No harpies.

HEARTS

VIRGO VESTALIS (PRIOR) PETIT AMANTEM PLATONICUM UT MAXIME CORRUMPATUR

Ex-Vestal Virgin seeks Platonic lover to spoil her rotten.

ESNE SOLUS SATURNALIBUS? CARESNE ALIQUA PROPRIA AD TEMPORA IUCUNDA COMMUNICANDA? TABERNA CONVENTUUM AMANTIUM, 'DUM ROMA ARDET' NOMINE, TIBI PRAEBEBIT AMANTEM QUEM IN SOMNIIS VIDERE VELIS

Alone for the Saturnalia? Missing that special someone to share the good times? "While Rome Burns" Dating Agency will set you up with the date of your dreams.

SIREN, PATRICIA ET FERVIDA, PETIT ALIQUEM INURBANUM. VICTIMAE DELECTAE SUNT GLADIATORES SCELESTIQUE (VENIAM CONFIRMARE POTEST).

Imperial Sultry Siren seeks a bit of rough. Preferred victims: gladiators and criminals (can guarantee pardon).

POCULUM SEMIPLENUM SEMIVACUUMVE EST? ROMANA ELEGENTISSIMA PETIT ALIQUEM BONAE SPEI QUOCUM MOMENTA EXIMIA COMMUNICET

Goblet half full? Or half empty? Rome's finest seeks optimist to share precious moments.

WOMEN SEEKING MEN

ARIES
TAURUS
GEMINI
CANCER
LEO
VIRGO
LIBRA
SCORPIO
SAGITTARIUS
CAPRICORNUS
AQUARIUS
PISCES
QUID EST TUUM SIDUS NATALICUM?
So what's your star sign?
MEA TABULA ASTROLOGICA PROMISIT ME HOC ANNO OCCURSURUM ALICUI SIMILI TIBI
My birth chart promised I would meet someone like you this year.
HOC SCIVI! EGO ETIAM
I knew it! Me too.

LOVE STARS

USE OUR HANDY LATIN ZODIAC CONVERTER ON THE FACING PAGE TO FILL IN THESE LINES AS APPROPRIATE:

FATUM EST!
It's Fate!

ACTA EIUSDEM TEMPORIS SALTEM SUNT, UT JUNGUS DICAT
Or at least synchronicity, as Jung would say!

SCILICET NON CREDO TALIBUS REBUS
Of course I don't really believe in all that stuff.

SED HARUSPEX ACTORUM DIURNORUM NOVI EBURACI NON MALUS EST
Though the soothsayer in the New York Times *is pretty good.*

DEBEO FATERI ME VALDE ATTRAHI ...
And I must admit I'm powerfully attracted to ...

APPARET UT ALIQUIS TAM FORMOSUS DEBEAT ESSE ...
It's obvious that someone as sexy as you MUST be a ...

NONNE ... EST SIDUS NATALICUM AMATORISSIMUM?
... is the most romantic sign, don't you think?

PRAECIPUE ATTINGENS ...
Particularly when it is on the cusp with ...

NUPTA ES? TALI! PER IOVEM, QUANTA FRUSTRATIO! TIBI NECESSE EST ...
You're married? To a ...? By Jupiter, what a shame! What you need is a ...

SIMILIS MIHI
Like me.

LOVE SPEAKS

NEC FACIEM, NEC TE PIGEAT LAUDARE CAPILLOS
ET TERETES DIGITOS EXIGUUMQUE PEDEM

Never grow tired of praising her face, her hair, her smooth fingers and slender feet.

OVID *ARS AMATORIA* 1.621-2

NERINE GALATEA, THYMO MIHI DULCIOR HYBLAE,
CANDIDIOR CYCNIS, HEDERA FORMOSIOR ALBA

Galatea, daughter of Nereus, sweeter to me than Hybla's thyme,
whiter than swans, more beautiful than pale ivy.

VIRGIL *ECLOGUES* 7.37-8

LILIA NON DOMINA SINT MAGIS ALBA MEA;
UT MAEOTICA NIX MINIO SI CERTET HIBERO,
UTQUE ROSAE PURO LACTE NATANT FOLIA

Lilies are no creamier than my mistress's skin;
like Maeotican snow competing with Spanish vermilion
or rose petals floating in pure milk.

PROPERTIUS 2.3.10-12

LESBIA FORMOSAST, QUAE CUM PULCHERRIMA TOTAST,
TUM OMNIBUS UNA OMNIS SURRIPUIT VENERES

Lesbia is beautiful, not only the loveliest of them all,
But she's the only one who's stolen all the allure
From all the rest.

CATULLUS 86.5-6

SWEET

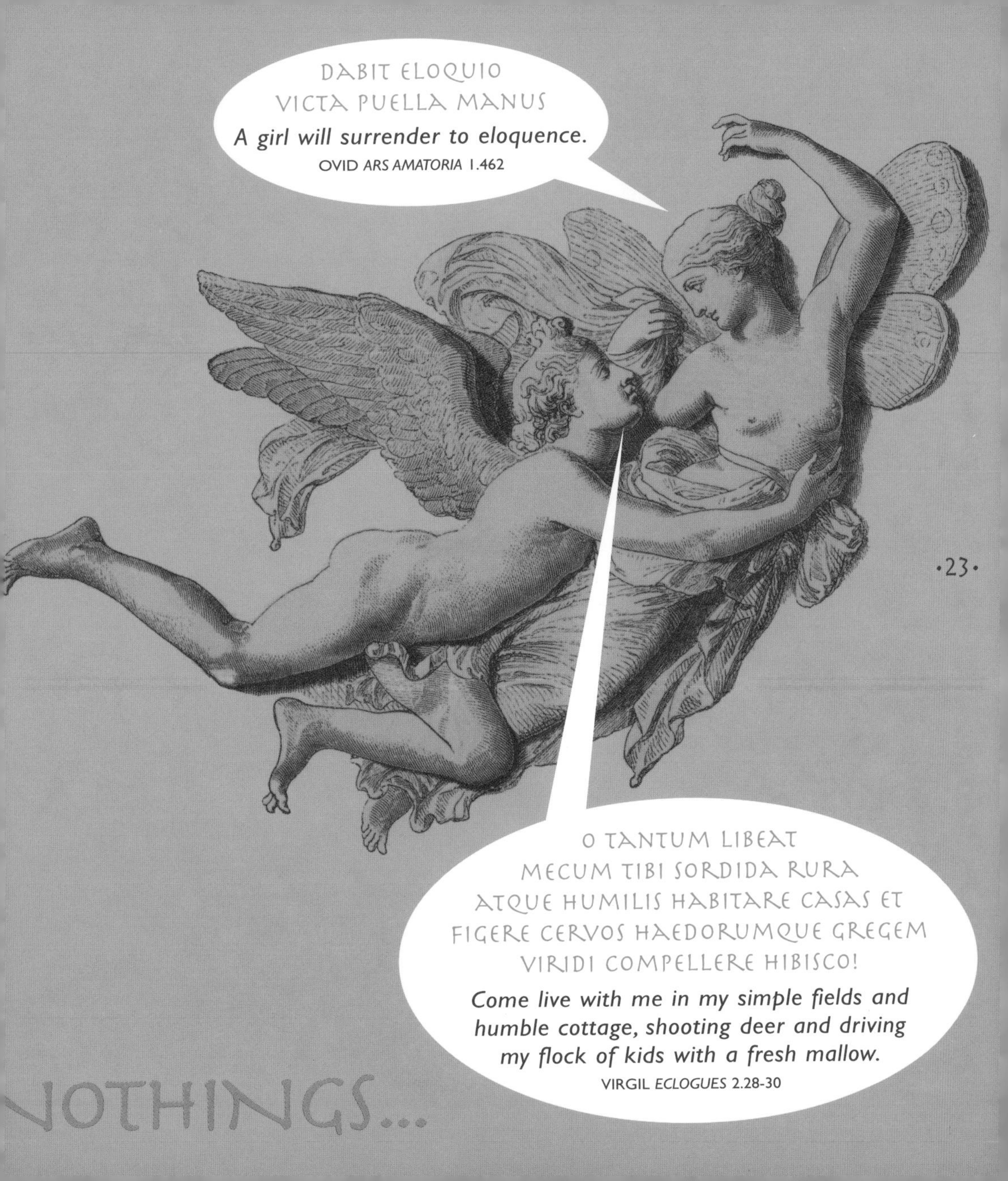
DABIT ELOQUIO
VICTA PUELLA MANUS
A girl will surrender to eloquence.
OVID ARS AMATORIA 1.462
O TANTUM LIBEAT
MECUM TIBI SORDIDA RURA
ATQUE HUMILIS HABITARE CASAS ET
FIGERE CERVOS HAEDORUMQUE GREGEM
VIRIDI COMPELLERE HIBISCO!
Come live with me in my simple fields and
humble cottage, shooting deer and driving
my flock of kids with a fresh mallow.
VIRGIL ECLOGUES 2.28-30
NOTHINGS...

LUCRETIUS, IN HIS DE RERUM NATURA, PARODIED THE LOVER'S REPERTOIRE OF INSINCERE HYPERBOLE ...

A swarthy one is "honey-coloured",

A foul and filthy one is "au naturelle",

A STRINGY AND WOODEN ONE IS "A GAZELLE",

A squat dwarf is "one of the Graces" and "full of wit",

A monstrous huge one is "phenomenal" and "full of grandeur",

If she stammers and can't speak, she has a "charming lisp",

A MUTE ONE IS "SHY",

A shameless, hateful chatterbox is "a little cracker",

One who looks starved to the point of death
is "a slender sweetheart",

ONE WITH FAT LIPS IS "ALL KISS".

ACCIPE, PER LONGOS TIBI QUI DESERVIAT ANNOS
Have me and I will be your slave for long years.
OVID AMORES 1.3.5

INVIDA VESTIS ERAS QUAE TAM BONA CRURA TEGEBAS
I'm jealous of that cloak of yours covering such gorgeous legs.
OVID AMORES 3.2.27

TU MIHI SOLA DOMUS, TU, CYNTHIA, SOLA PARENTES,
OMNIA TU NOSTRAE TEMPORA LAETITIAE
You alone are my home, Cynthia, you my parents,
you my every moment of happiness.
PROPERTIUS 1.11.23-4

SIT MIHI PAUPERTAS TECUM IUCUNDA, NEAERA:
AT SINE TE REGUM MUNERA NULLA VOLO
With you, Neaera, poverty would be bliss.
Without you I wouldn't want a king's ransom.
LYGDAMUS 3.3.23-4

NON MIHI MILLE PLACENT, NON SUM DESULTOR AMORIS
I'm not after a thousand girls at once,
I don't sleep around.
OVID AMORES 1.3.15

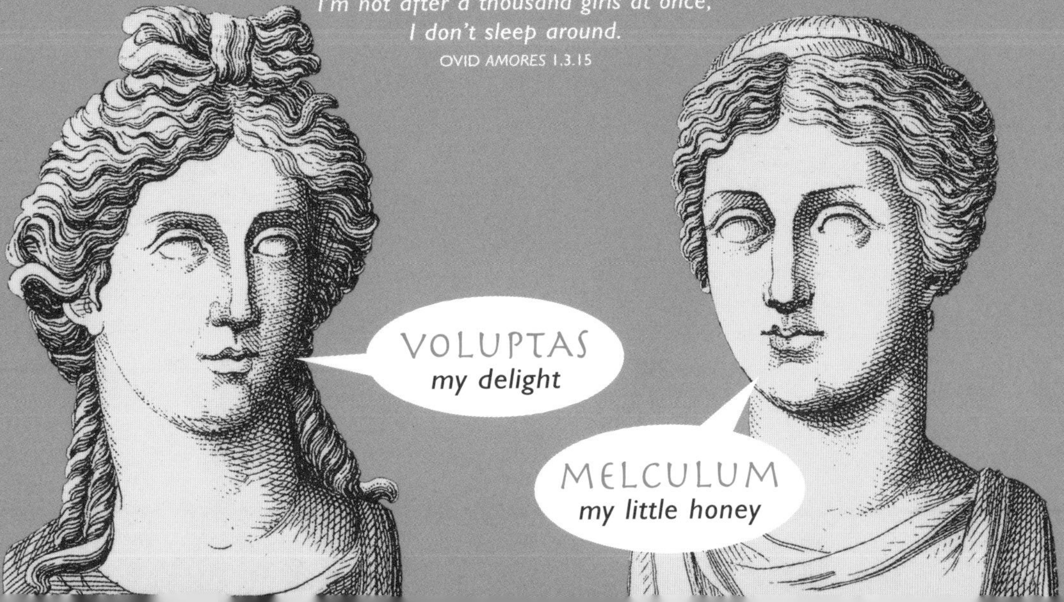

VOLUPTAS
my delight

MELCULUM
my little honey

DUM LOQUIMUR,
FUGERIT INVIDA AETAS:
CARPE DIEM

While we're speaking jealous time flies: seize the day.

HORACE *ODES* 1.11.7-8

QUID SIT FUTURUM
CRAS, FUGE QUAERERE ET
QUEM FORS DIERUM CUMQUE DABIT,
LUCRO APPONE NEC DULCES AMORES
SPERNE PUER NEQUE TU CHOREAS

Don't ask what will happen tomorrow,
Whatever the sum of days given to you,
Think of it as treasure,
And when you are young,
Never say no to dancing and sweet desire.

HORACE *ODES* 1.9, 13-16

RISIT ET ARGUTIS QUIDDAM PROMISIT OCELLIS

She smiled and made a certain promise with her speaking eyes.

OVID AMORES 3.2.83

CARPE DIEM

TEMPTA HAS OSTREAS MANIBUS COLLECTAS. ITA FACILE LANGUESCES
Try some of these hand-dived oysters. They'll help you unwind.

NUM AMATORIUM MEDICAMENTUM EST? PLANE NESCII
Surely not! An aphrodisiac? I had no idea.

FORTASSE HAEC CEREBRA OVIUM? MODO APPIANO PARATA SUNT
Or perhaps these sheep's brains? They're done the Appian way (a main road out of Rome).

MODO IOCOR
Only joking.

PLUS FALERNI?
More Falernian? (a kind of wine)

MIHI PLACET TUAM DOMUM VIDERE. DOMUS TANTA DE ALIQUO PATEFACIUNT
I'd love to see your house. Houses tell you so much about a person.

PRAECIPUE CUBICULA
Particularly bedrooms.

ERGO APUD ME?
My place, then?

NON MULTUM EST SED MEA DOMUS EST
It ain't much, but it's home.

ITA VERO, MEA PALAESTRA PRIVATA EST
Yes, that's my private gym.

ITA VERO, ET VETUSTA ROMANA ET FEMINAS FORMOSAS / VIROS FORMOSOS COLLIGO
Yes, I collect Roman antiquities and beautiful women/men.

INDUAM MODO ALIQUID PAULUM COMMODIUS
I'll just slip into something a little more comfortable.

TIBI PLACEAT UTI BALNEO EFFERVESCENTI/MERSO
Feel free to use the jacuzzi/sunken bath.

QUOD REFUGIT, MULTAE CUPIUNT: ODERE QUOD INSTAT
Many girls lust after what they can't get and hate what's offered on a plate.
OVID *ARS AMATORIA* 1.717

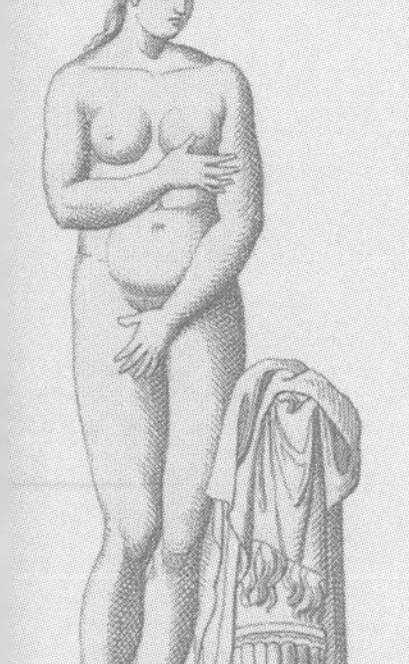

...TANTUM CUPIT
ILLA ROGARI
She's dying to be asked.
OVID *ARS AMATORIA* 1.711

NEMPE NOS CERTE AMANTES
IN PRIORE VITA FUIMUS
You know, I'm sure we were lovers in another life.

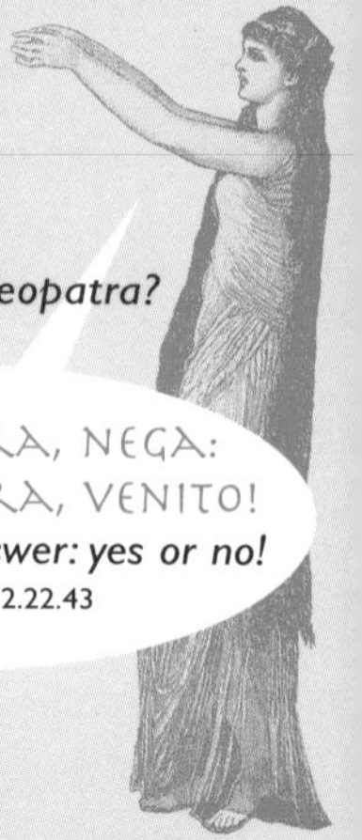

FORTASSE ROMAE ANTIQUAE ANTONIUS
CLEOPATRAQUE FUIMUS?
Perhaps in ancient Rome we were Antony and Cleopatra?

AUT CAESAR CLEOPATRAQUE?
Or Caesar and Cleopatra?

AUT SI ES DURA, NEGA:
SIN ES NON DURA, VENITO!
Just give me an answer: yes or no!
PROPERTIUS 2.22.43

AUT PTOLEMAEUS CLEOPATRAQUE?
Or Ptolemy and Cleopatra?

IMMO, NON PUTO TE FIDEM FALLERE
No, I don't think you sleep around.

NOLI ROGARE QUID ROMANI PRO TE FACERENT,
ANIMA MEA: ROGA QUID TU PRO ROMANIS FACERE POSSIS
Don't ask what the Romans did for you, darling: ask what you can do for the Romans.

ILLE PERFECTUS MORTUUS EST. QUAM AD REM ADSUESCERE DEBES.
A ME SUBSTITUTUS EST
Mr Right is dead. Get used to it. I'm his replacement.

ACHILLES SUM IN FORO ET PRIAPUS IN CUBICULO/
DIANA SUM IN CURIA ET VENUS IN CUBICULO
I'm Achilles on the trading floor and Priapus in the bedroom/
Diana in the boardroom and Venus in the bedroom.

NOLI TE NOXIUM AESTIMARE. SINE INFIDELITATE,
NEQUE LITTERAE NEQUE FABULAE TOGATAE ESSENT
Don't feel guilty. Without infidelity, there would be
no literature or soap operas!

QUIS SCIT QUID CRAS FIAT
Who knows what tomorrow will bring?

VIX A TE VIDEOR
POSSE TENERE MANUS!
I can hardly seem to keep my
hands off you!
OVID *AMORES* 1.4.10

SCIS TE ID MAXIME VELLE
You know you want to.

TE ORO!
Please!

ITA VERO, RES MAGNI MOMENTI CRAS FACIAM.
TIBINE PLACEBIT MATURE CUBITUM IRE?
OK, I have a big day tomorrow too. How about an early night?

QUID DICIS? VIS EVENTUM MEAE PROBATIONIS SAPERE?
What do you mean, you want to see my test results?

SCILICET TE AMO. MAGIS QUAM MARE AEGAEUM
Of course I love you. More than the Aegean Sea.

ITA VERO, TE ETIAM CRAS MANE MAGNI AESTIMABO
YES, I will still respect you in the morning.

ESNE FRIGIDUS/FRIGIDA?
Are you frigid?

AMOR
ODIT INERTES
Love hates slow movers.
OVID *ARS AMATORIA* 2.229

SOLANE PERPETUA MAERENS CARPERE IUVENTA,
NEC DULCIS NATOS VENERIS NEC PRAEMIA NORIS?
Will you spend your whole youth alone and sad,
not knowing sweet children or the rewards of Venus?
VIRGIL *AENEID* 4.32-3

IAM SUBREPET INERS AETAS, NEC AMARE DECEBIT,
DICERE NEC CANO BLANDITIAS CAPITE
Sluggish old age will creep up on you before you know it:
it won't be dignified to love or flirt with a white head.
TIBULLUS 1.1.71-2

... SI PERTENDENS ANIMO VESTITA CUBARIS
SCISSA VESTE MEAS EXPERIERE MANUS
If you persist in lying fully clothed you'll feel
my hands tear your clothes off.
PROPERTIUS 2.15.17-18

PLUS IN
MORA PERICULI
There is danger in delay.
LIVY *HISTORIES* 38.25.13

DESINE DISSIMULARE; DEUS CRUDELIUS
URIT, QUOS VIDET INVITOS SUCCUBUISSE SIBI
Stop pretending. The Love God burns more
fiercely for those he sees put up a fight.
TIBULLUS 1.8.7-8

STUPID CUPID

ETSI ULTIMUS VIR/
ULTIMA FEMINA IN TOTO
ORBE TERRARUM ESSES
*Not if you were the last man/
woman on earth.*

IN SOMNIIS!
In your dreams!

ETSI DUAS HORAS VITAE HABEREM
Not if I had two hours to live.

IMMO, ETSI DUAS HORAS VITAE HABERES
No, not if you had two hours to live.

MALIM LINGUA MEA CLOACAM MAXIMAM PURGARE
I'd rather lick the Cloaca Maxima (Rome's sewer) clean.

... VEL STABULA AUGEAE DETERGERE
Or scrub out the Augean stables (one of the labours of Hercules).

SENTENTIAE TUAE MATRIS/TUI PATRIS MANIFESTE
NON EAEDEM ERANT
Clearly not the position your mother/father took.

ALIQUIS ME IAM POSTULAVIT. HOMO SAPIENS
I'm already spoken for. By a human being.

NON EST MIHI CURA ETSI SIBYLLA CUMAEA NOSTRAM
CONIUNCTIONEM PRAEDIXISSET
I don't care if the Sibyl of Cumae predicted our union.

NEMO EST QUIN ERRET
Everyone makes mistakes.

NOLI ME TANGERE
Leave me alone.

ME PAENITET
QUOD CUM ALTERO
GENERE CONIUNGI NOLO
*Sorry, I don't mate outside
my species*

TE MONEO. MEUS PATRUUS
SICILIANUS EST ET MEI CONSOBRINI CENTURIONES SUNT
*I'm warning you, my uncle comes from Sicily
and my cousins are centurions.*

THE PARACLAUSITHYRON OR SHUT DOOR POEM WAS A COMMON FEATURE OF LATIN LOVE POETRY. IT DESCRIBES THE POET SHUT OUT OF HIS LOVER'S HOUSE, LAMENTING HER CRUELTY AND BEGGING FOR ADMITTANCE.

LOCKED DOOR LAMENTS

NAM POSITA EST NOSTRAE CUSTODIA SAEVA PUELLAE, CLAUDITUR ET DURA IANUA FIRMA SERA. IANUA DIFFICILIS DOMINI, TE VERBERET IMBER, TE IOVIS IMPERIO FULMINA MISSA PETANT. IANUA, IAM PATEAS UNI MIHI VICTA QUERELLIS, NEU FURTIM VERSO CARDINE APERTA SONES

A cruel watch has been put on my girl and the hard-hearted door has been firmly locked in my face. Oh door of a stubborn master, may the rain pelt you and lightning sent by Jove target you! Oh door give in to my complaints, open just to me and make no sound as you turn your stealthy hinge.

TIBULLUS 1.2.5-10

FERREUS ORANTEM NEQUIQUAM, IANITOR, AUDIS

You listen to my hopeless begging like iron, door-keeper.

OVID *AMORES* 1.6.27

... ADITU FAC IANUA PARVO OBLIQUUM CAPIAT SEMIADAPERTA LATUS. LONGUS AMOR TALES CORPUS TENUAVIT IN USUS

Open the door ajar so I can slip through the little crack sideways. My long love has wasted away my body for just such uses.

OVID *AMORES* 1.6.3-5

AT LACRIMANS EXCLUSUS AMATOR LIMINA SAEPE FLORIBUS ET SERTIS OPERIT POSTISQUE SUPERBOS UNGUIT AMARACINO ET FORIBUS MISER OSCULA FIGIT

The weeping shut-out lover often buries the threshold in flowers and garlands, anoints the proud doorposts with marjoram scent and plants miserable kisses on the door.

LUCRETIUS *DE RERUM NATURA* 4.1177-9

OBSTACLES

SI INTERDICTA PETES, VALLO CIRCUMDATA (NAM TE
HOC FACIT INSANUM), MULTAE TIBI TUM OFFICIENT RES,
CUSTODES, LECTICA, CINIFLONES, PARASITAE,
AD TALOS STOLA DEMISSA ET CIRCUMDATA PALLA,
PLURIMA QUAE INVIDEANT PURE APPARERE TIBI REM

If you lust after what's forbidden and defended on all sides (for this is what drives you crazy with desire), all sorts of things then get in your way: guards, sedan chairs, hair-dressers, hangers-on, her ankle-length dress and unrevealing cloak, a thousand things that begrudge you a clear view.

HORACE *SATIRES* 1.2.96-100

SOME MORE ADVICE FROM OVID'S ARS AMATORIA ON HOW TO AVOID AND EXPLOIT THE OBSTACLES TO LOVE.

How will a chaperone stop you writing a love letter when it's bath time?

3.619-20

... OR WHEN A CONFIDANTE CAN CARRY YOUR WRITTEN TABLET IN HER BRA AGAINST HER WARM BOSOM?

3.621-2

... or when she can hide the tied paper in her sock
and the sexy message in her shoe?

3.623

*Let it also be your aim to suck up to your girl's husband:
he'll be more useful to you as a friend.*

1.579-80

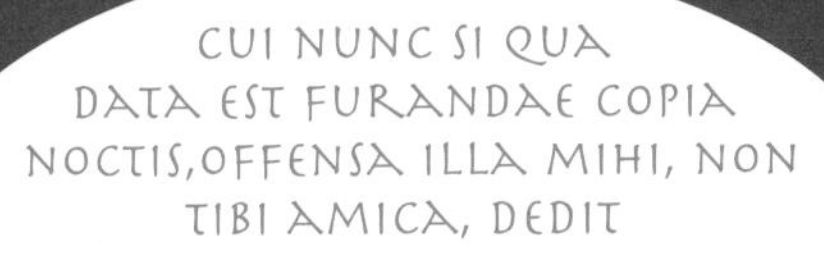

CUI NUNC SI QUA
DATA EST FURANDAE COPIA
NOCTIS,OFFENSA ILLA MIHI, NON
TIBI AMICA, DEDIT

If you were granted a stolen night of pleasure, it was only because she was pissed with me, not in love with you.

PROPERTIUS 3.8.39-40

ILLE PER EXCUBIAS CUSTODUM
LENITER IRE MONSTRAT

Love shows me how to tiptoe past the guard watch.

OVID *AMORES* 1.6.7-8

AT TU PER PRAECEPS TECTO DELABERE
APERTO: DET QUOQUE FURTIVAS ALTA
FENESTRA VIAS. LAETA ERIT, ET
CAUSAM TIBI SE SCIET ESSE PERICLI

Slide in head first through a gap in the roof or let a high window give you a cheeky way in. She'll be happy knowing you've put yourself in danger all for her.

OVID *ARS AMATORIA* 2.245-7

QUOD LICET, INGRATUM EST; QUOD
NON LICET ACRIUS URIT

What is permitted does nothing for me; what is forbidden arouses more fiercely.

OVID *AMORES* 2.19.3

OSCULATIONS

ILLA LICET NON DET, NON DATA SUME TAMEN

Although she doesn't give them, take the kisses she doesn't give.

OVID *ARS AMATORIA* 1.664

ADFIGUNT AVIDE CORPUS IUNGUNTQUE SALIVAS ORIS ET INSPIRANT PRESSANTES DENTIBUS ORA

Lovers cling greedily with their bodies and join their wet mouths, draw deep breaths biting each other's mouths.

LUCRETIUS *DE RERUM NATURA* 4.1108-9

OSCULA QUI SUMPSIT, SI NON ET CETERA SUMET,
HAEC QUOQUE, QUAE DATA SUNT, PERDERE DIGNUS ERIT

The man who kisses but doesn't go all the way didn't even deserve the kiss.

OVID *ARS AMATORIA* 1.669-70

TRIA GENERA OSCULANTIUM: MACHINA EXSTINGENS, HOMO MORTUUS ARTE MEDICATUS ET MACHINA EXSORBENS

There are three kinds of kissers: the fire extinguisher, the mummy and the vacuum cleaner.

HELEN GURNEY BROWN

THE KISSING POET

CATULLUS (84–54 BC) WAS FAMOUS FOR HIS KISSING POEMS DEDICATED TO HIS ARISTOCRATIC MISTRESS, LESBIA, PROBABLY CLODIA METELLI. HERE ARE SOME EXTRACTS.

GIVE ME A THOUSAND KISSES, AND THEN A
HUNDRED, THEN ANOTHER THOUSAND,
AND THEN A SECOND HUNDRED...

To kiss you with so many kisses,
with some left over,
Will just about satisfy Catullus,
mad with love ...

*You ask me how many of
your kisses, Lesbia, would be
enough to satisfy me, with
some left over.
They would need to be
of the same number
as the grains of Libyan sand
Thrown up on the spicy shores
of Cyrene ...*

I SNATCHED, WHILE YOU
PLAYED, SWEET-AS-HONEY,
A KISS SWEETER THAN
SWEET AMBROSIA ...

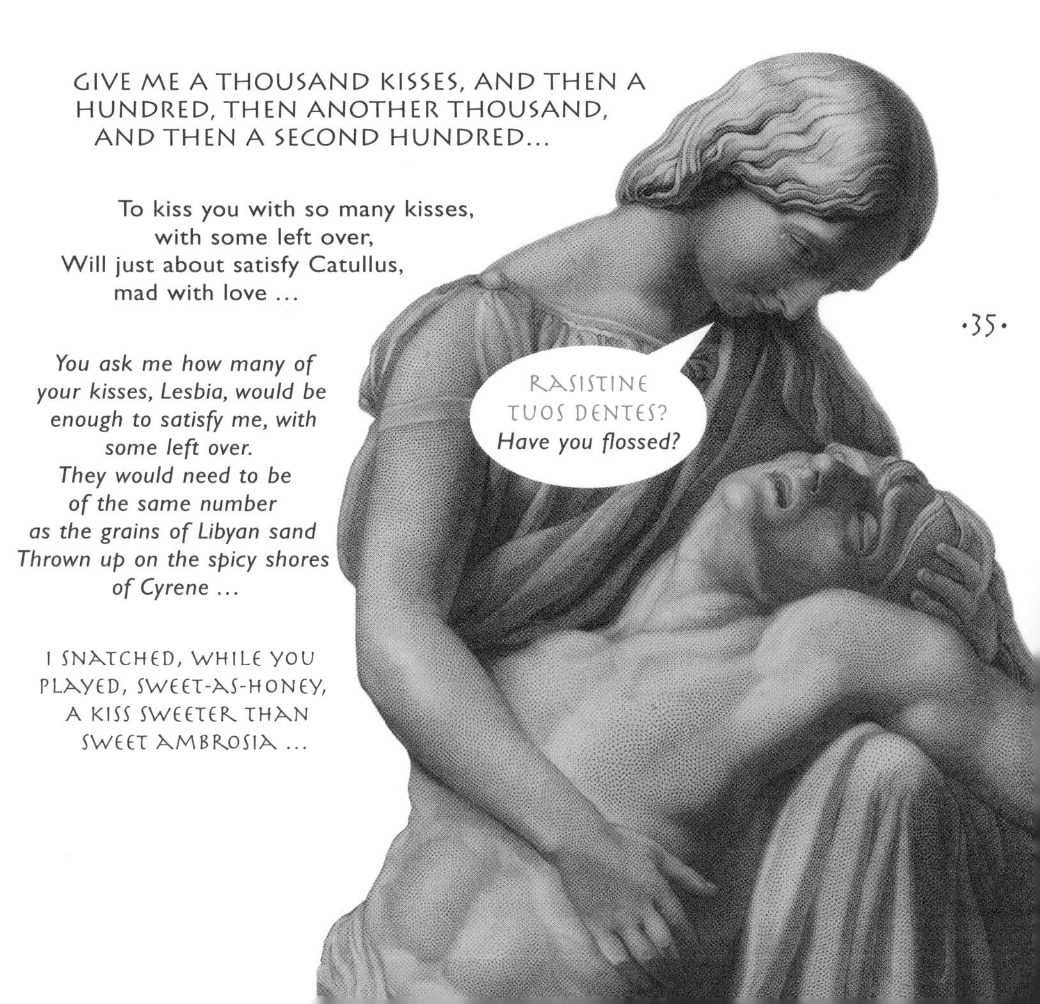
RASISTINE
TUOS DENTES?
Have you flossed?

ADVANCED

EVEN THE ROMANS HAD THEIR EUPHEMISMS – LITERAL TRANSLATIONS ARE IN BRACKETS

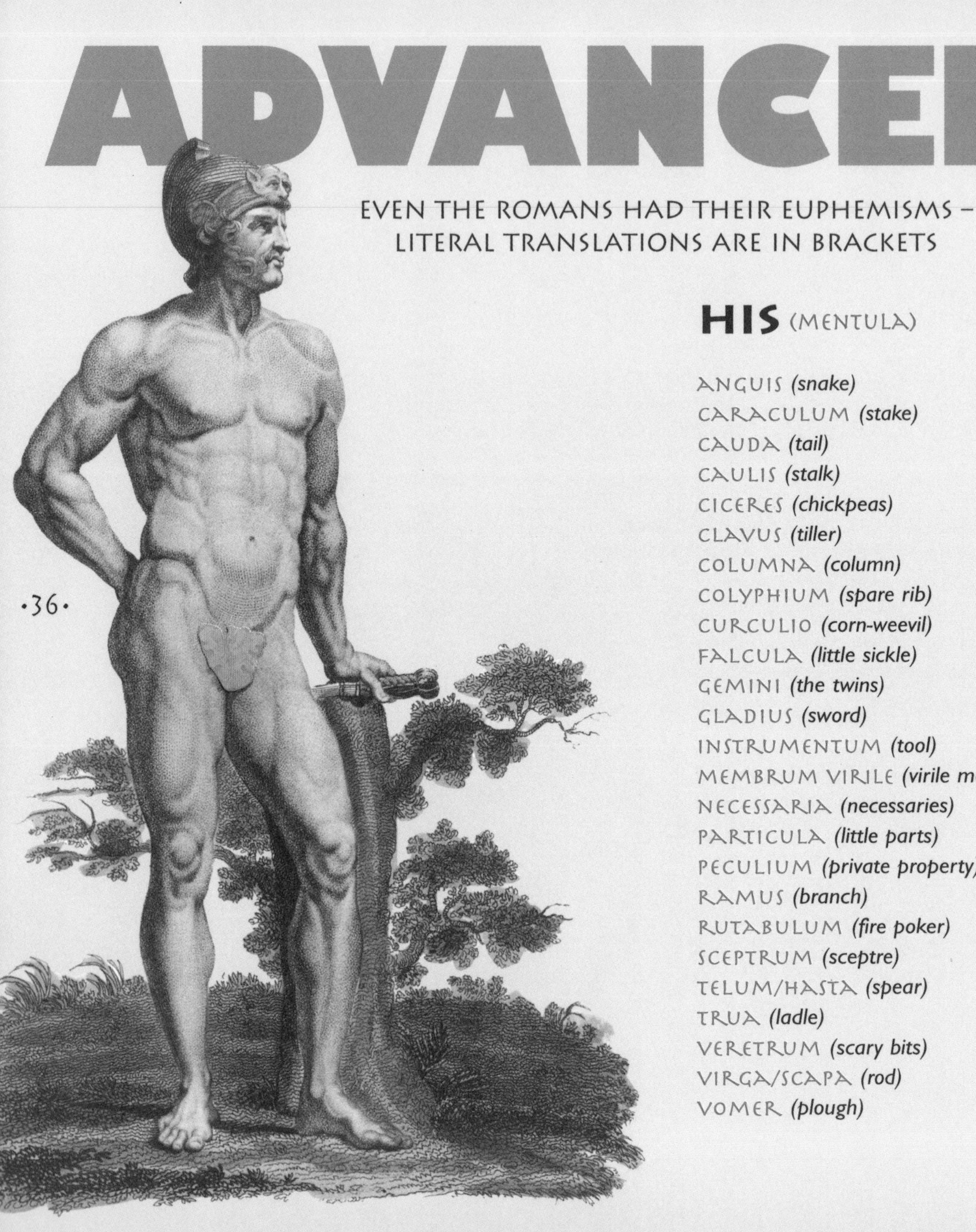

HIS (MENTULA)

ANGUIS *(snake)*
CARACULUM *(stake)*
CAUDA *(tail)*
CAULIS *(stalk)*
CICERES *(chickpeas)*
CLAVUS *(tiller)*
COLUMNA *(column)*
COLYPHIUM *(spare rib)*
CURCULIO *(corn-weevil)*
FALCULA *(little sickle)*
GEMINI *(the twins)*
GLADIUS *(sword)*
INSTRUMENTUM *(tool)*
MEMBRUM VIRILE *(virile member)*
NECESSARIA *(necessaries)*
PARTICULA *(little parts)*
PECULIUM *(private property)*
RAMUS *(branch)*
RUTABULUM *(fire poker)*
SCEPTRUM *(sceptre)*
TELUM/HASTA *(spear)*
TRUA *(ladle)*
VERETRUM *(scary bits)*
VIRGA/SCAPA *(rod)*
VOMER *(plough)*

VOCABULARY

WAYS & MEANS (FACIO)

ESSE CUM *(be with)*
DORMIO CUM *(sleep with)*
CONCUMBO *(to lie with)*
MISCEO *(mix)*
IOCARI/LUDERE *(fool around)*
FODIO DIGITO *(fondle)*
EXCAVO *(excavate)*
LIGURIO *(lick)*
SUCULO *(suck)*
BIBO *(drink)*
VORO *(devour)*
TRAICIO *(pierce)*
OPERAM DO *(to be on the job)*
ARO *(plough)*
DEPSO *(knead)*
MOLO *(grind)*
SEDO *(ride)*
BATTUO/TUNDO/PULSO *(bang)*
SUBIGO *(master)*
AD METAM PROPERO *(hurry to the goal)*
SERO *(sow the seed)*
PATRIO/PERFICIO/PERVENIO/
CONFICIO *(climax)*

HERS (CUNNUS)

AGER *(field)*
ARA *(altar)*
ARVUS *(field)*
BULGUS *(leather bag)*
CRISTA *(crest)*
FOVEA *(pit)*
HUMUS *(earth)*
IANUA *(door)*
LIMEN *(threshold)*
NASUS *(nose)*
NAVIS *(ship)*
PARTES MULIEBRES *(ladies' bits)*
PINNACULA *(little wings)*
PISCINA *(swimming pool)*
PORCELLINA *(piggie)*
SPECUS *(cave)*
SULCUS *(furrow)*
VAGINA *(sword sheath)*

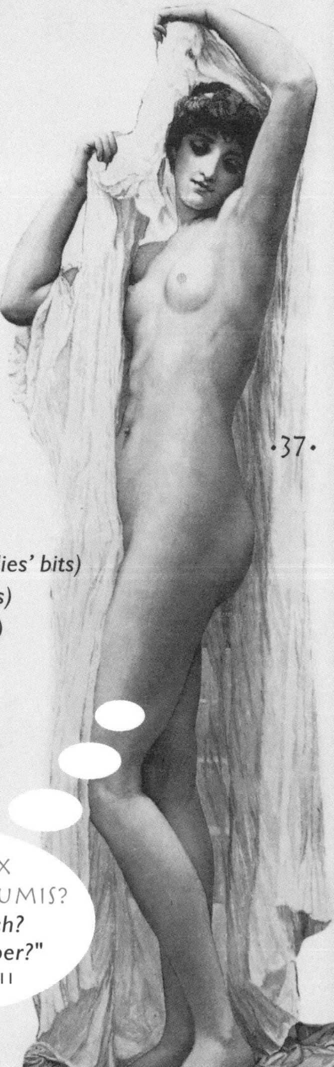

NUM RADIX
FUIT? NUM CUCUMIS?
*"Was it a radish?
Was it a cucumber?"*
PLAUTUS *CASINA* 911

RED-HOT

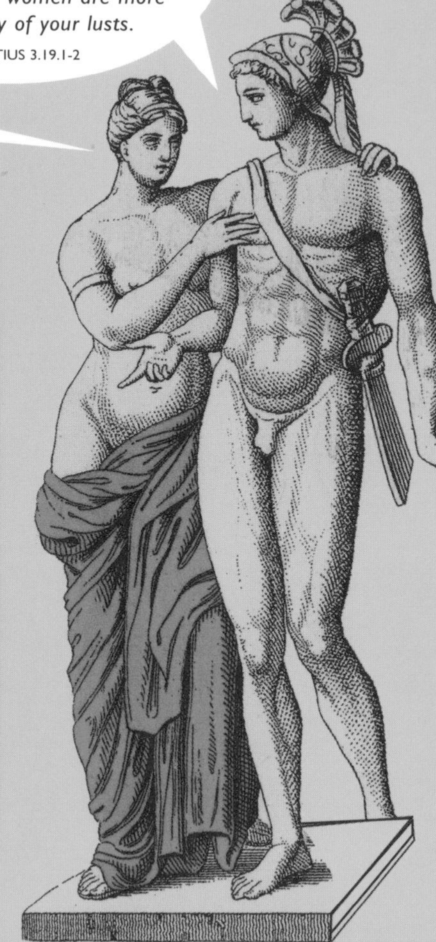

OBICITUR TOTIENS A TE MIHI NOSTRA LIBIDO: CREDE MIHI, VOBIS IMPERAT ISTA MAGIS
You often blame the male libido but believe me, you women are more at the mercy of your lusts.
PROPERTIUS 3.19.1-2
QUARE ETIAM ATQUE ETIAM, UT DICO, EST COMMUNI' VOLUPTAS
So I say again and again, pleasure is for both parties.
LUCRETIUS *DE RERUM NATURA* 4.1208

SOME TIPS AND TECHNIQUES FROM OVID:

Older women make love in a thousand ways according to your taste: more positions than you could find in any manual.

ARS AMATORIA 2.679-80

I LIKE TO SEE SURRENDER IN THE EYES OF A FRENZIED MISTRESS.

ARS AMATORIA 2.691-2

Enjoy the sex and moment of bliss but make sure you shout out what fun you're having.

ARS AMATORIA 2.307-8

WHEN YOU'RE FAKING IT, JUST BE CAREFUL NOT TO MAKE IT OBVIOUS.

ARS AMATORIA 3.801

LATIN LOVING

TIBINE SE MOVIT ORBIS TERRARUM?
Did the earth move for you?

LACRIMASNE?
Is that a tear in your eye?

NOLI SOLLICITARI, OMNIBUS IDEM OCCURRERE POTEST
That's OK, it happens to everyone.

PARVULA! PARVULA! PARVULA!
Baby, Baby, Baby!

POSSIM TE EXESSE!
I could just eat you up!

QUAM SUAVIS!
Yum yum!

EVAX!
Oooh!

TE FIRMA!
Brace yourself!

VESUVIUS!
Vesuvius!

ITA!
ITA!
ITA!
Yes!
Yes!
Yes!

If you've got a stunning face, lie on your back.
ARS AMATORIA 3.773
Let each woman know herself ... one position does not suit all.
ARS AMATORIA 3.771-2

OVID'S ADVICE

I will teach you in which way a woman is to be loved.

ARS AMATORIA 3.28

THE LEFT HAND SHOULD NOT LIE IDLE ON THE BED.

ARS AMATORIA 2.706

The fingers will find what to do in those parts in which Love secretly dips his darts.

ARS AMATORIA 2.707-8

WHEN YOU'VE FOUND WHERE A WOMAN LIKES TO BE TOUCHED,
DON'T BE EMBARRASSED TO TOUCH IT.

ARS AMATORIA 2.719-20

While she struggled, as if she didn't want to be overcome,
she was overcome – it wasn't very hard – by her own betrayal.

AMORES 1.5.15-16

Skill makes love last forever.

ARS AMATORIA 3.42

When we're up against each other she's any Ilia or Egeria to me.
HORACE *SATIRES* 1.2.125-6
Ilia, vestal virgin mother of Rome's founder Romulus, and Egeria, the nymph wife of Numa, second king of Rome, are figures from Roman mythology.

Don't stop with the seductive sighs and pleasurable murmurs.

***ARS AMATORIA* 3.795**

DON'T STIFLE THE KINKY WORDS WHILE YOU'RE PLAYING.

***ARS AMATORIA* 3.796**

I like it when her screams betray her pleasure and she begs me to slow down and hold back.

***ARS AMATORIA* 2.689-90**

TRUST ME:

DON'T RUSH THE CLIMAX.

ARS AMATORIA 2.717

But when it's dangerous to hang about, go full steam ahead and spur the galloping horse.

ARS AMATORIA 2.731-2

Don't spread too much sail and leave her behind nor let her finish the race first. Score your goal at the same time then, satisfied, you can lie, overcome, together.

ARS AMATORIA 2.725-8

LET A WOMAN FEEL THE EARTH MOVE, UNSTRUNG TO THE CORE OF HER BONES.

ARS AMATORIA 3.793-4

You'll see her eyes shining a blissful gleam just as the sun often sparkles on clear water.

ARS AMATORIA 2.721-2

MUSICAL INTERLUDE

HOC POTEST INITIUM ALICUIUS MAGNI ESSE
This Could Be The Start Of Something Big.

ME COMMOVE, ME REFRIGERA, ME EXPLE
Thrill Me, Chill Me, Fulfil Me.

LANGUESCE, NOLI ID FACERE
Relax, Don't Do It.

EGO ET TU, AMICULA, MODO ANIMALIA SUMUS
You And I, Baby, Ain't Nothing But Mammals.

DIC MIHI QUID VELIS, QUID VERE, VERE, VELIS
Tell Me What You Want, What You Really, Really, Want.

ALIQUID ME DOCET ME IN ALIQUO
BONO LAPSUM ESSE
Something Tells Me I'm Into Something Good.

TE TENEO SUB MEA CUTE
I've Got You Under My Skin.

GIFTS OF LOVE

ADFERAT IN CALATHO RUSTICA DONA PUER. RURE SUBURBANO POTERIS TIBI DICERE MISSA, ILLA VEL IN SACRA SINT LICET EMPTA VIA

Let a slave take her some rustic presents in a basket. You can say they were sent to you from your suburban estate even though you bought them on the Sacred Way.

OVID *ARS AMATORIA* 2.264-6

CANDIDUS, ALCATHOI QUI MITTITUR URBE PELASGA, BULBUS ET, EX HORTO QUAE VENIT, HERBA SALAX OVAQUE SUMANTUR, SUMANTUR HYMETTIA MELLA, QUASQUE TULIT FOLIO PINUS ACUTA NUCES

Let her eat white onions, sent from the Pelasgian city of Alcathous, and that aphrodisiac herb which comes from the garden and eggs and Hymettus honey and the nuts which the sharp-leafed pine tree bears.

OVID *ARS AMATORIA* 2.421-4

NEC DOMINAM IUBEO PRETIOSO MUNERE DONES: PARVA SED E PARVIS CALLIDUS APTA DATO

Don't give your mistress expensive presents. Be smart: choose things that are small but suitable.

OVID *ARS AMATORIA* 2.261-2

FELIX QUI VILES POMIS MERCARIS AMORES!

You lucky man who can buy love cheaply for apples!

PROPERTIUS 2.34.71

SERVUS ET AD PARTES SOLLERS ANCILLA PARENTUR, QUI DOCEANT, APTE QUID TIBI POSSIT EMI

Get a slave and maid primed for the role to point out suitable gifts he can buy for you.

OVID *AMORES* 1.8.87-8

CUM TE DEFICIENT POSCENDI MUNERA CAUSAE, NATALEM LIBO TESTIFICARE TUUM

When all other pretexts for asking for presents have failed, bake a cake to hint that it's your birthday.

OVID *AMORES* 1.8.93-4

MUNERA PRAECIPUE VIDEAT, QUAE MISERIT ALTER. SI DEDERIT NEMO, SACRA ROGANDA VIA EST

Let him especially see presents another man has sent. If no-one has, go out and get something on the Sacred Way.

OVID *AMORES* 1.8.99-100

SWEETS FOR MY SWEET, SUGAR FOR MY HONEY: LATIN LOVE GIFTS

The following presents will show the sensitivity of Latin Lovers with a range of budgets.

BARGAIN BASEMENT

WHITE PEBBLE
(signifying a happy day)

QUINCE
(often celebrated in love poems)

PINE NUTS
(cited by Ovid as an aphrodisiac)

BOUTIQUE

HYMETTUS HONEY
(this Greek honey was particularly flavorsome and admired for its pale color)

STONE PHALLUS
(brought good luck)

OIL LAMP WITH SUGGESTIVE ILLUSTRATIONS
(terracotta oil lamps with erotic decoration were very popular)

TIFFANY'S

MALTESE WHITE PUPPY
(portrayed in mosaics and described in poetry)

SARDONYX CAMEO
(prized and valuable in ancient Rome)

CONGRATULATIONS

IMMORTALIS ERO
SI ALTERA TALIS ERIT

Another night like that and I'll live forever.
PROPERTIUS 2.14.10

VERUM GAUDIUM RES SEVERA EST
True joy is a serious thing.
SENECA *EPISTULAE* 23.4.5-6

QUAM MULTA APPOSITA NARRAMUS VERBA LUCERNA,
QUANTAQUE SUBLATO LUMINE RIXA FUIT!
How we flirted while the lights were on
and how we rolled around when they were off!
PROPERTIUS 2.15.3-4

NOCTE UNA QUIVIS
VEL DEUS ESSE POTEST
One night like that can make any man a god.
PROPERTIUS 2.15.40

QUALIS NOX FUIT ILLA, DI DEAEQUE,
QUAM MOLLIS TORUS. HAESIMUS CALENTES
ET TRANSFUDIMUS HINC ET HINC LABELLIS
ERRANTES ANIMAS. VALETE,
CURAE MORTALES
Gods and goddesses, what a night that was! How soft was the bed!
We stuck together with our heat and exchanged our
wandering souls, our lips everywhere. Farewell earthly cares!
PETRONIUS *SATYRICON* 79

... MIHI SI SECUM TALES CONCEDERE NOCTES
ILLA VELIT, VITAE LONGUS ET ANNUS ERIT
If she wants to give me more nights like that,
a year will be a long life for me.
PROPERTIUS 2.15.37-8

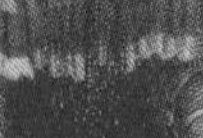

HOW DO I LOVE THEE?

A LATIN VOCABULARY FOR COUNTING THE WAYS

OMNINO
Completely

STUDIOSE
Devotedly

INSANE
Madly

ARDENTI MENTE
Inextinguishably

SOLUM
Exclusively

MODO DOMINI
Possessively

SERVILITER
Slavishly

INDULGENTER
Tenderly

DULCITER
Sweetly

MODO POETARUM
Poetically

IOCOSE
Playfully

AVIDE
Hungrily

MODO CUSTODIS
Protectively

ARDENTER
Passionately

LIBIDINOSE
Lasciviously

SITIENTER
Thirstily

MUSICAL INTERLUDE

NUMQUAM ALTERUM AMEM
It Had To Be You.

TU ES MIHI OMNIA
All The Things You Are.

A AMABILIS ES (CARMEN LITTERARUM)
A You're Adorable (The Alphabet Song).

CORPUS ANIMAQUE
Body And Soul.

TE AMO, TE CANDIDE AMO
I Love You, I Honestly Love You.

HOC IAM DIUTISSIME NON FACTUM EST
This Hasn't Happened For The Longest Time.

IMPROPER SUG

IT'S ALL TOO EASY FOR LATIN LOVERS TO COME UP WITH HOWLERS. HERE ARE SOME PHRASES TO USE WITH CARE. THE CORRECT TRANSLATION IS IN BRACKETS.

IN FLAGRANTE DELICTO
Dumping rubbish in broad daylight.
(Caught in the act)

COITUS INTERRUPTUS
Acclaimed poet of the Silver Age, unable to finish his masterwork.
(Interrupted in the act)

AD HOC
Shall we change to white wine then?
(As and when)

NIL DESPERANDUM
The Norwegian hasn't had it for months.
(Despair at nothing)

AD NAUSEAM
I'm allergic to monotonous sex.
(To the point of sickening boredom)

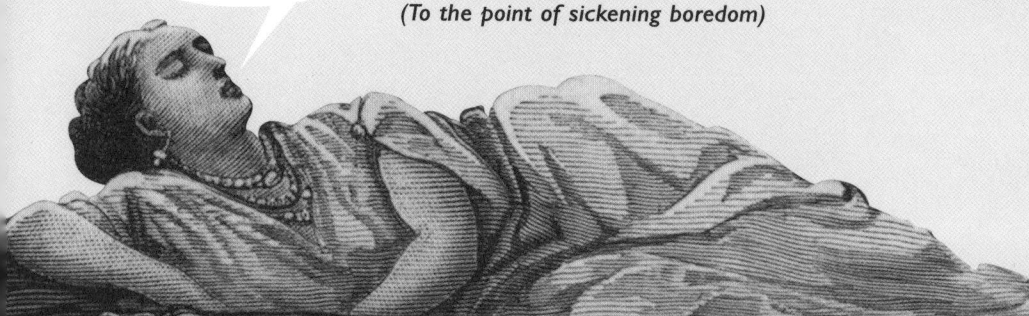
EHEU!
Hey you, fancy a quickie?
(Alas!)

GESTIONS

MAE WEST

THE AMERICAN ACTRESS MAE WEST (1893–1980) COINED AN UNFAIR SHARE OF THE MOST PROVOCATIVE HOLLYWOOD ONE-LINERS. WE HAVE ADAPTED SOME FOR THE MODERN LATIN LOVER.

HORA MATUTINA SURGENDUM EST QUI VESTES LANEAS CAPERE VELIT, SERO VIGILANDUM QUI VESTEM SERICAM

You gotta get up early in the morning to catch a fox and stay up late at night to get a mink.

Mink was unknown to the Romans so we have taken the liberty of substituting "woollies" and "silk" for fox and mink.

ESTNE FASCINUM QUOD IN TUA TUNICA VIDEO VEL ME VIDERE TIBI PLACET?

s that an amulet in your tunic or are you just pleased to see me?

SI MANUM VIRI LIBERAS, TIBI TOTUM CORPUS MULCEBIT

Give a man a free hand and he'll run it all over you.

NONNULLI VIRI INCULTISSIMI OPTIMAE DELICIAE FIUNT

Some of the wildest men make the best pets.

UNUS VIR DOMI VALET EIUSDEM PRETII QUAM IN VIA DUO

A man in the house is worth two in the street.

UBI DIXERUNT DECEM VIROS EAM DOMI OBVIAM IVISSE, "DEFESSA SUM," INQUIT, "MITTE DOMUM UNUM."

On being told that ten men were waiting to meet her at her home: "I'm tired, send one of them home."

NIVEA ERAM SED LAPSA SUM

I used to be Snow White but I drifted.

ASCENDE OLIM AD ME VIDENDAM
Come up and see me sometime.

SUSPICIOUS MINDS

NOVIMUS ET QUI TE, TRANSVERSA TUENTIBUS HIRCIS

We know what you were up to while your goats looked the other way.

VIRGIL *ECLOGUES* 3.8

SAEPE VIRI FALLUNT: TENERAE NON SAEPE PUELLAE

Men deceive often, gentle girls don't.

OVID *ARS AMATORIA* 3.31

MUSICAL INTERLUDE

SINGING THE BLUES

NOLI FRANGERE MEUM PECTUS

Don't Go Breaking My Heart.

IN SOMNO LOQUEBARIS

You've Been Talking In Your Sleep.

AMISISTI CONSUETUDINEM AMANTIS

You've Lost That Loving Feeling.

QUID TE ATTIGIT?

What In The World Came Over You?

NUMQUAM TIBI HORTUM PLENUM ROSARUM PROMISI

I Never Promised You A Rose Garden.

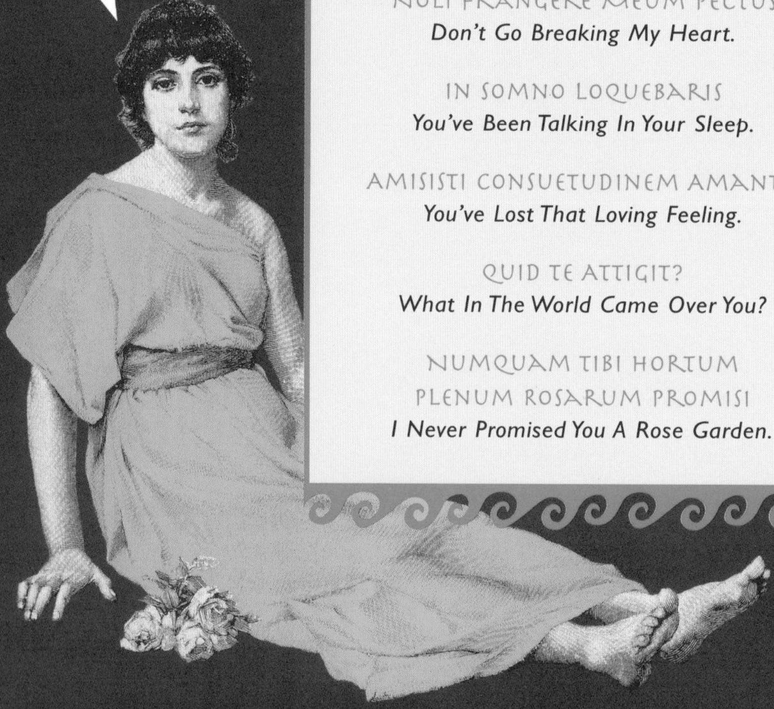

VOTA MORI MEA SUNT,
CUM TE PECCARE RECORDOR

*When I think you've cheated on me,
I pray for death.*

OVID *AMORES* 2.5.3

IPSE MISER DOCUI, QUO POSSET LUDERE PACTO
CUSTODES: EHEU, NUNC PREMOR ARTE MEA

*I, poor wretch, taught her how to trick her watchers:
now, alas, I'm suffering from my own cleverness.*

TIBULLUS 1.6.9-10

... NIHIL EST AUDACIUS ILLIS
DEPRENSIS: IRAM ATQUE ANIMOS A
CRIMINE SUMUNT

*Nothing is as brazen as a woman caught in the act:
her guilty conscience increases her fury.*

JUVENAL *SATIRES* 6.284-5

SIQUAM LAUDAVI MISERO PETIS
UNGUE CAPILLOS;SI CULPO, CRIMEN
DISSIMULARE PUTAS

*If I compliment another girl I'm in for it
as you fly at my hair with your claws out.
If I criticize her you think I'm hiding something.*

OVID *AMORES* 2.7.7-8

... NON TAM LATERA ECFUTUTA PANDAS,
NI TU QUID FACIAS INEPTIARUM

*You wouldn't show such shagged-out shanks
if you weren't up to no good.*

CATULLUS 6.13-14

TE DECEAT MEDIO IURA DEDISSE FORO

*Let it suit you to throw the rule book at me
as if we were in court.*

OVID *AMORES* 2.17.24

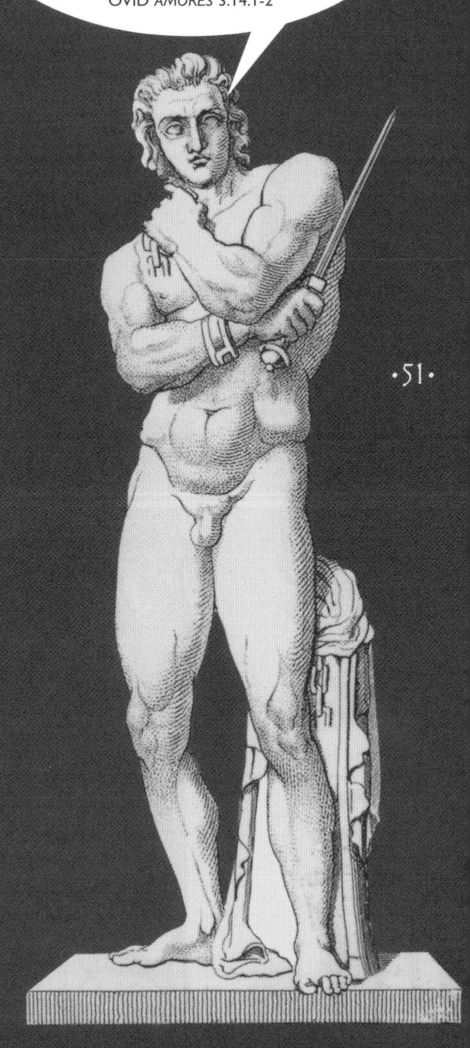

NON EGO NE
PECCES, CUM SIS FORMOSA,
RECUSO SED NE SIT MISERO SCIRE
NECESSE MIHI
I don't blame you for cheating – you're
gorgeous – I'm miserable because I
have to find out about it.
OVID AMORES 3.14.1-2

LOVE HURTS

IN MORSO AEQUALES
VIDEANT MEA VULNERA COLLO:
ME DOCEAT LIVOR MECUM HABUISSE MEAM
I want my friends to see the love-bites on my neck;
let the bruises show what a good night I've had.
PROPERTIUS 3.8.21-2

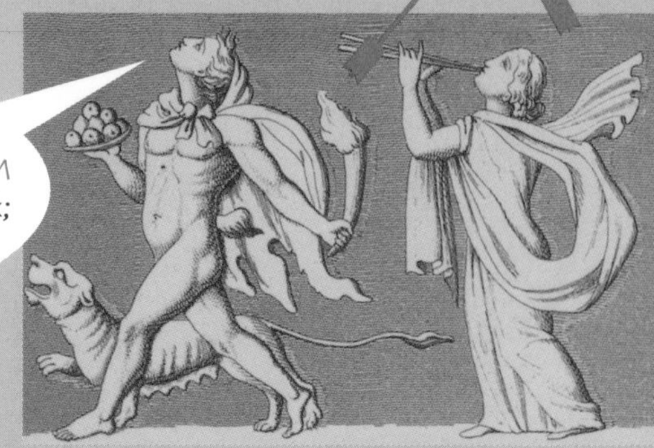

UNA AUT ALTERA NOX NONDUM EST IN AMORE PERACTA,
ET DICOR LECTO IAM GRAVIS ESSE TUO
We've not even spent one or two nights making love
and you're already telling me I'm a pain in bed.
PROPERTIUS 2.24.19-20

HOSTIS SI QUIS ERIT NOBIS, AMET ILLE PUELLAS
Let my enemies fall in love.
PROPERTIUS 2.4.17

ODERO SI POTERO; SI NON, INVITUS AMABO
I will hate if I can. If not, I will unwillingly love.
OVID *AMORES* 3.11.35

AVERSOR MORUM CRIMINA – CORPUS AMO
I hate what you are but I love what I see.
OVID *AMORES* 3.11.38

ODI ET AMO. QUARE ID FACIAM, FORTASSE REQUIRES.
NESCIO, SED FIERI SENTIO ET EXCRUCIOR
I hate and I love. Perhaps you'll ask why?
I don't know. But I feel it happening, and it's crucifying me.
CATULLUS 85

NEC ME CONTUMELIAE LASSANT: QUOD VERBERATUS SUM, NESCIO; QUOD EIECTUS SUM, LUSUM PUTO. MODO REDIRE IN GRATIAM LICEAT

I don't get tired of the insults. I forget about the beatings. I think it's fun to be thrown out. Just let me back into her good books!

PETRONIUS *SATYRICON* 138

LUCTANTUR PECTUSQUE LEVE IN CONTRARIA TENDUNT
HAC AMOR HAC ODIUM, SED, PUTO, VINCIT AMOR

Love and Hate are embroiled in a tug-of-war in my heart. I think Love will win.

OVID *AMORES* 3.11.33-4

DULCIS AD HESTERNAS
FUERAT MIHI RIXA LUCERNAS,
VOCIS ET INSANAE TOT MALEDICTA TUAE

I loved the lamplight brawl we had last night, especially the appalling abuse from your maddened tongue.

PROPERTIUS 3.8.1-2

QUAE MULIER
RABIDA IACTAT CONVICIA
LINGUA,HAEC VENERIS MAGNAE
VOLVITUR ANTE PEDES

The woman who hurls raging curses is in fact lying helpless at great Venus's feet.

PROPERTIUS 3.8.11-12

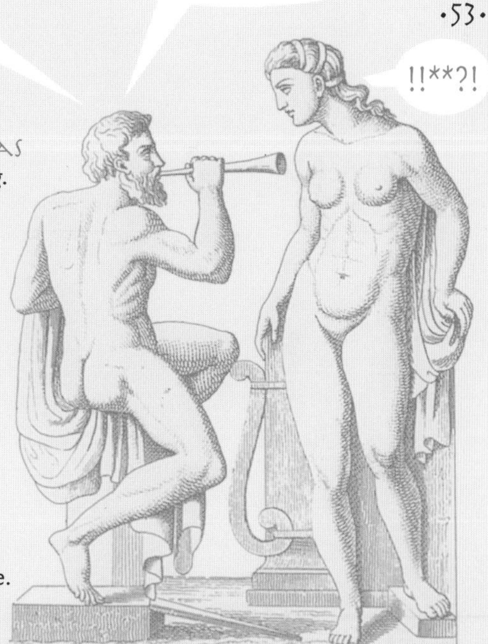

EST QUAEDAM FLERE VOLUPTAS

There's a certain pleasure in crying.

OVID *TRISTIA* 4.3.37

DIFFICILIS FACILIS, IUCUNDUS
ACERBUS ES IDEM:NEC TECUM
POSSUM VIVERE NEC SINE TE

At the same time
Impossible and irresistible,
Silk and steel,
I can't live with you, or without you.

MARTIAL *EPIGRAMS* 12.47

AMANTIUM IRAE
AMORIS INTEGRATIO EST

Lovers' quarrels are the renewal of love.

TERENCE *ANDRIA* 555

FIFTY WAYS TO LE

OVID'S REMEDIA AMORIS OR REMEDIES TO LOVE WAS PUBLISHED IN 1 BC AS AN ANTIDOTE TO THE ARS AMATORIA. THE FOLLOWING EXTRACTS TEACH THE LOVER HOW TO LEAVE HIS MISTRESS AND FALL OUT OF LOVE.

I *Where you can, make the worst of her charms.*
325

II *Don't list her faults in case she puts them right.*
695

III *If she has bad teeth, tell her something to make her laugh.*
339

IV *Is she all breast up top? Get her not to wear a bra.*
337-8

V *If she's honest, call her simple.*
330

VI *Whatever she's useless at, coax her into doing it.*
331-2

VII *It'll also help to rush to her house in the morning as a surprise before she's put her face on.*
341-2

AVE YOUR LOVER

VIII *Go look at her face (don't be shy) when she's painting it with her poisonous concoctions. They've turned my stomach more than once.*
351-2, 356

IX *Choose a position for sex that you think will look least attractive.*
407-8

X *Open all the windows so her body is unflattered by the natural light.*
411-12

TUO AMORE
NON DIGNUS SUM
You're too good for me.

XI *When you're lying there afterwards, knackered in body and mind, make a mental note of any blemish on her body.*
414, 417

TE AMO,
SED NON DEPERIRE
I love you, but I'm not in love with you.

XII *Go with someone else first so you're too shagged to get enthusiastic about her.*
401-2

XIII *Beware of girlie tears: they've trained their eyes to cry.*
689-90

XIV *Is her door open? Walk on by although she calls you back.*
519

XV *Has she invited you over? Find something else in your diary for that night.*
520

XVI *Laugh when you should be in tears.*
494

XVII *Pretend – although it's not the case – that you've given up your passion.*
497

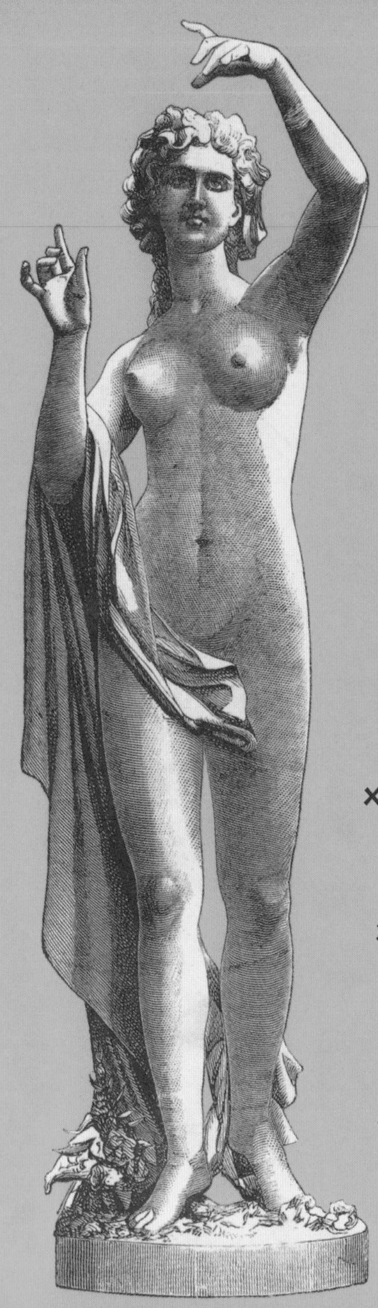

XVIII *Don't wheedle her round;*
don't hurl abuse at her door;
don't lie down on her hard doorstep.
507-8

XIX *Don't let her slave or her little maid*
come to you with crocodile tears.
639

XX *Tell her to keep the presents you gave her*
without argument.
671

XXI *Don't ask how she is even if you want to know.*
641

XXII *Don't trouble to please your ex.*
Make sure she's now just one of many.
681-2

XXIII *Have two girls on the go at once*
(anyone who can handle more is quite a man).
441-2

XXIV *For whoever's in love quiet places are dangerous.*
Avoid quiet places! Where are you going?
There's safety in numbers.
579

XXV *Don't avoid socializing; don't shut everyone out;*
don't sit in the dark and cry.
587-8

XXVI *This is where friends come in really useful.*
590

XXVII *Keep on remembering what that cow of a girl*
has done and keep all your losses in your mind's eye.
299-300

XXVIII *Don't reread the seductive, treasured letters she sent you:*
put them all (painfully) on a fierce fire.
717, 719

XXIX *If you can bear it, get rid of pictures of her.*
Why are you captivated by a mute image?
723-4

XXX *Loathe as I am to say it: don't touch the love poets!*
757

XXXI *Don't picture any rival to yourself.*
Believe she's lying on her bed alone.
769-70

PERFECTI SUMUS, IAMDUDUM PERFECTI
We're history. Ancient history.

MIRABILE ERAT
It's been amazing.

SPERO NOS FAMILIARES MANSUROS
I hope we can still be friends.

POTES ANULUM/SERVUM/CENTURIONEM/RAMUM OLEAE SERVARE
You can keep the ring/slave/centurion/olive branch.

XXXII *It's hopeless defending against a passion for the girl next door; best to avoid the neighborhood.*
625-6

XXXIII *Don't stroll down that colonnade where she likes to stroll.*
627-8

XXXIV *Greet the man you once loathed as a rival. When you can do so with affection, you're cured.*
791, 794

XXXV *Aim for total sobriety or drunkenness beyond caring. Anything in between is dangerous.*
809-10

XXXVI *Places are often dangerous. Shun those places that have witnessed your love-making.*
725-6

XXXVII *Don't meet up with mutual friends.*
628

MUSICAL INTERLUDE

QUO CESSIT NOSTER AMOR?
Where Did Our Love Go?

SUPERABO
I Will Survive.

UBI FERIAE PERACTAE SUNT
When The Carnival Is Over.

IMMITTE SCURRAS
Send In The Clowns.

NUMQUAM ALTERUM TE INVENIAM
I'll Never Find Another You.

ET BENE CONFIXUM MENTO DISCUSSERIS UNCUM, NIL ERIT HOC: ROSTRO TE PREMET ANSA SUO

It's no good shaking out the hook that's fixed fast in your chin: you'll still be dangling on the end of her line.

PROPERTIUS 4.1.141-2

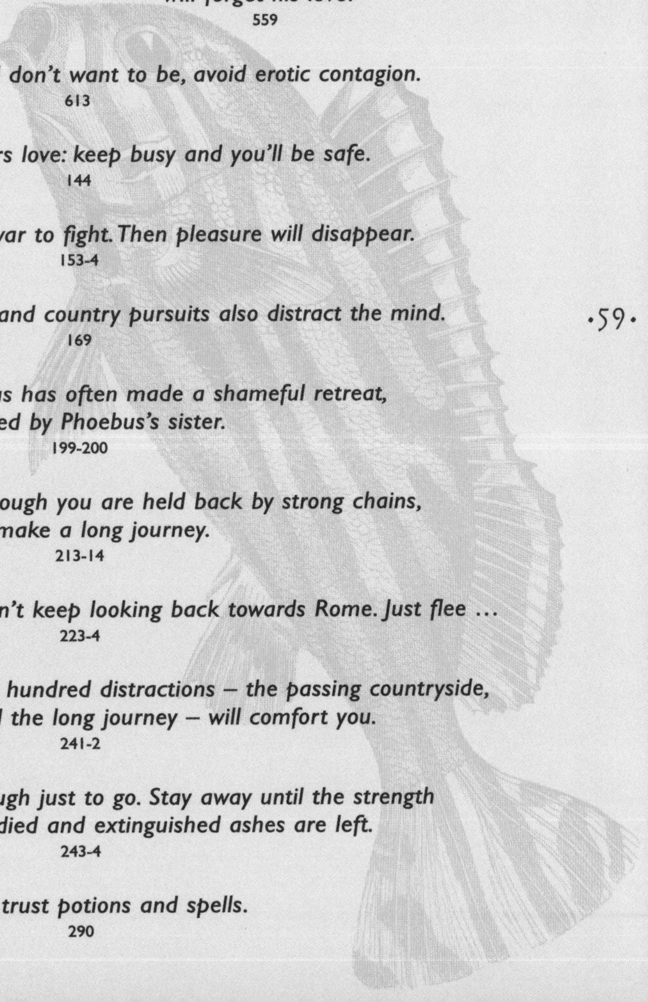

XXXVIII *Try to get sick of your affliction: weariness brings an end to love.*
539

XXXIX *Love lingers long that diffidence feeds.*
543

XL *Whoever thinks about his own problems will forget his love.*
559

XLI *If you're in love and don't want to be, avoid erotic contagion.*
613

XLII *Work conquers love: keep busy and you'll be safe.*
144

XLIII *Find yourself a war to fight. Then pleasure will disappear.*
153-4

XLIV *The great outdoors and country pursuits also distract the mind.*
169

XLV *Go hunting: Venus has often made a shameful retreat, defeated by Phoebus's sister.*
199-200

XLVI *Go travelling, although you are held back by strong chains, and make a long journey.*
213-14

XLVII *Don't count the days, don't keep looking back towards Rome. Just flee …*
223-4

XLVIII *Once you've set off, a hundred distractions – the passing countryside, your companions and the long journey – will comfort you.*
241-2

XLIX *Don't think it enough just to go. Stay away until the strength of your passion has died and extinguished ashes are left.*
243-4

L *Don't trust potions and spells.*
290

FINALES

... NE FORTE TUO CAREAT MIHI FUNUS AMORE,
HIC TIMOR EST IPSIS DURIOR EXSEQUIIS

That I might die without your love is a harsher fear than death itself.

PROPERTIUS 1.19.3-4

TECUM VIVERE AMEM, TECUM OBEAM LIBENS

With you I would live, with you I would die.

HORACE *ODES* 3.9.24

TE SPECTEM, SUPREMA MIHI CUM VENERIT HORA;
TE TENEAM MORIENS DEFICIENTE MANU

Let it be you I look at when my final hour comes and you I hold in my failing embrace as I die.

TIBULLUS 1.1.59-62

AUFERAT HORA DUOS EADEM, NEC CONIUGIS UMQUAM
BUSTA MEAE VIDEAM, NEU SIM TUMULANDUS AB ILLA

May the same hour take us both; may I neither see my wife's tomb nor be put in mine by her.

OVID *METAMORPHOSES* 8.709-10

SI NON URNA, TAMEN IUNGET NOS LITTERA: SI NON
OSSIBUS OSSA MEIS, AT NOMEN NOMINE TANGAM

If we cannot share an urn,
let us share an epitaph:
if our bones may not embrace,
let our names.

OVID *METAMORPHOSES* 11.706-7

HUIUS ERO VIVUS,
MORTUUS HUIUS ERO
I will be hers in life and hers in death.
PROPERTIUS 2.15.36

FOREVERS

CRAS AMET QUI NUMQUAM AMAVIT;
QUIQUE AMAVIT, CRAS AMET

Tomorrow let those who have never loved, love;
Let those who have loved, love tomorrow.

TIBERIANUS (ATTRIB.) *PERVIGILIUM VENERIS*

... VASTO LABENTUR FLUMINA PONTO,
ANNUS ET INVERSAS DUXERIT ANTE VICES,
QUAM TUA SUB NOSTRO MUTETUR PECTORE CURA

Rivers will flow upstream from the vast sea and the year will reverse its seasons
before my love for you will change in my heart.

PROPERTIUS 1.15.29-31

UNUM LITUS ERIT SOPITIS UNAQUE TECTO
ARBOR, ET EX UNA SAEPE BIBEMUS AQUA;
ET TABULA UNA DUOS POTERIT COMPONERE AMANTIS

We shall share
A single shore for sleep,
A single tree for shelter,
And often we will drink
From a single spring,
And a single narrow bed
Will hold both lovers.

PROPERTIUS 2.26.31-3

AMOR ANIMI ARBITRIO SUMITUR, NON PONITUR
We choose to love but not to stop loving.
PUBLILIUS SYRUS SENTENTIAE 5
NON SATIS EST ULLO TEMPORE LONGUS AMOR
However long it lasts, Love never lasts long enough.
PROPERTIUS 1.19.26

GODS

VENUS *Goddess of Love, Beauty and Fertility. She was a Patron Goddess of the city of Rome because her son, Aeneas, was one of the founders of the city.*

CUPID *The little son of Venus. He was depicted as winged and mischievous, armed with a bow and arrows that would cause those they wounded to fall in love.*

DIANA *Sister of the God Phoebus Apollo. She was usually represented as a virgin huntress, though her worship was also associated with Fertility and Childbirth.*

PRIAPUS *God of Fertility. Commonly depicted with an obscenely large phallus.*

JOVE/JUPITER *King of the gods.*

HEROES

ACHILLES. *Greatest Greek hero who fought in the Trojan War and defeated the Trojan prince Hector. Died before the end of the war from a poisoned arrow in the heel.*

ANTONY *(Marcus Antonius) (c. 82–30 BC). Ruled Rome alongside Octavian (later the emperor Augustus Caesar) until his defeat at the battle of Actium. Committed suicide with his lover Cleopatra (see below).*

CAESAR *(Gaius Julius Caesar) (100–44 BC). Aristocrat who became dictator of Rome before being assassinated by the Republican senators. He founded the first dynasty of Roman emperors.*

CLEOPATRA *(69–30 BC). Queen of Egypt and lover of Antony with whom she committed suicide with an asp after being defeated by Octavian.*

CYNTHIA *Girlfriend of Propertius (see below).*

EPICURUS *(341–271 BC). Athenian philosopher. His ethical theory was based on pleasure as the sole good.*

NEARA *Girlfriend of Lygdamus (see below).*

PTOLEMY *Name given to the members of a great dynasty of kings of Egypt.*

SYBIL OF CUMAE *Prophetess thought to be inspired by the God of Prophecy, Apollo. Cumae is in the volcanic area around Naples, southwest Italy.*

AND POETS

CATULLUS *(Gaius Valerius Catullus) (c. 84–54 BC). Roman love poet. His most famous poems concern his stormy affair with "Lesbia" who was almost certainly the notorious Clodia, wife of Quintus Metellus Celer.*

CICERO *(Marcus Tullius Cicero) (106–43 BC). Roman politician and orator. Outspoken supporter of the Republic which resulted in his murder by Octavian, who later became the emperor Augustus.*

HORACE *(Quintus Horatius Flaccus) (65–8 BC). Roman poet. His Odes were on a variety of subjects.*

JUVENAL *(Decimus Junius Juvenalis) (1st–2nd century AD). Roman satirist.*

LIVY *(Titus Livius) (59 BC–AD 17). Roman historian. Wrote a history of Rome from before its foundation to his own time.*

LUCRETIUS *(Titus Lucretius Carus) (94–55 BC). Roman philosopher. His philosophy was based on the teachings of Epicurus (see above).*

LYGDAMUS *(fl. late 1st century BC). Roman love poet. The six surviving elegies of Lygdamus were preserved with the poems of Tibullus.*

OVID *(Publius Ovidius Naso) (43 BC–c. AD 18). Roman poet. Ovid was exiled to the Black Sea when his lascivious writings about love fell into disfavour with the emperor Augustus.*

PETRONIUS *(Titus Petronius Arbiter) (d. AD 65). Roman writer. His Satyricon is a portrait of decadent life in the 1st century of the Roman empire. The most famous section of the book concerns a wildly extravagant and depraved dinner party given by the vulgar millionaire Trimalchio.*

PLAUTUS *(Titus Maccius Plautus) (fl. 204–184 BC). Roman comic playwright.*

PROPERTIUS *(Sextus Propertius) (c. 50–c. 15 BC). Roman love poet. His poems were mostly dedicated to "Cynthia", who was probably his real-life mistress, Hostia.*

PUBLIUS SYRUS *(fl. 1st century BC). Writer of comic mime plays. Only a collection of sententiae ("proverbs") remains, thought to be taken from his plays.*

MANILIUS *(fl. early 1st century AD). Roman poet. Wrote a poetic treatise on the constellations.*

MARTIAL *(Marcus Valerius Martialis) (c. AD 40–103). Roman poet. Wrote epigrams on a variety of light-hearted subjects.*

SENECA *(Lucius Annaeus Seneca) (fl. early 1st century AD). Roman philosopher and tragic playwright. Part of the imperial court. Tutored the young emperor Nero by whom he was eventually forced to commit suicide.*

TERENCE *(Publius Terentius Afer) (fl. 166–159 BC). Roman comic playwright.*

TIBULLUS *(Albius Tibullus) (c. 55–c. 19 BC). Roman love poet. His love poems were mostly dedicated to "Delia" whose real name was probably Plancia.*

VIRGIL *(Publius Vergilius Maro) (70–19 BC). Roman poet. Wrote a variety of poems on the Italian countryside and a long epic on the original founder of Rome, Aeneas.*

accipe,
per longos tibi qui
deserviat annos

Have me and I will be your slave for long years.

OVID *AMORES* 1.3.5

ERGO

Vix a te videor
posse tenere manus!

I can hardly seem to keep my hands off you!

OVID *AMORES* 1.4.10

IUVAT INCONCESSA
VOLUPTAS

Forbidden pleasure delights.

OVID *AMORES* 3.4.31